UP, DOWN, AND SIDEWAYS

UP, DOWN, AND SIDEWAYS:

High-Impact Verbal Communication for HR Professionals

Patricia M. Buhler, SPHR, and Joel D. Worden

Society for Human Resource
Management

Alexandria, Virginia

www.shrm.org

Strategic Human Resource
Management India

Mumbai, India

www.shrmindia.org

Society for Human Resource
Management

Haidian District Beijing, China

www.shrm.org/cn

This book is published by the Society for Human Resource Management (SHRM®). The interpretations, conclusions, and recommendations in this book are those of the authors and do not necessarily represent those of the publisher.

The Society for Human Resource Management (SHRM) is the world's largest association devoted to human resource management. Representing more than 250,000 members in over 140 countries, the Society serves the needs of HR professionals and advances the interests of the HR profession. Founded in 1948, SHRM has more than 575 affiliated chapters within the United States and subsidiary offices in China and India. Visit SHRM Online at www.shrm.org.

Interior Design: Jihee Kang Lombardi
Cover Design: Jihee Kang Lombardi

Library of Congress Cataloging-in-Publication Data

Buhler, Patricia M.

  Up, down, and sideways : high-impact verbal communication for HR professionals / Patricia M.

Buhler, SPHR, DBA and Joel D. Worden, Ph.D.

  pages cm

Includes bibliographical references and index.

ISBN 978-1-58644-337-5

1. Communication in personnel management. I. Worden, Joel D., 1977- II. Title.

HF5549.5.C6B785 2013

658.3001'4–dc23

2013004952

13-0100

Contents

Chapter 1

Introduction: The Case for Effective Communication

People everywhere admire the ant for its industry and efficiency. The tiny insects work so well as a team that they can carry off the proverbial picnic lunch before you know it. That kind of teamwork depends on one primary skill: communication.

In fact, every complex system depends on clear communication. Consider, for instance, an analogy to the human body. What makes your eyes scan this sentence, your lungs expand with air, or your fingers turn this page? Communication. Sure, it's neurological instead of verbal, but it's strong, healthy communication nonetheless. We could have the legs of a world-class marathoner, but if our spinal cord—the chief means of communication with our body—were severed, those legs would do us no good. We would have a healthy mind and robust legs, yet be unable to accomplish our goals, all because of ineffective communication from our mind to our legs.

Just as communication is at the heart of the body's mechanisms and the ant's industry, so it is at the heart of good business. The best idea or the slickest new product will never go far without great communication, as has been shown in study after study.

Everybody Loves a Good Communicator

David Grossman reported in "The Cost of Poor Communications" that a survey of 400 companies with 100,000 employees each cited an average loss per company of $62.4 million per year because of inadequate communication to and between employees.[1]

Additionally, the Towers Watson *2009/2010 Communication ROI Study Report* found that "effective employee communication is a leading indicator of financial performance and a driver of employee engagement. Companies that are highly effective communicators had 47 percent higher total returns to shareholders over the last five years compared with firms that are the least effective communicators."[2] Forty-seven percent higher returns to shareholders—what our companies would not give to make that happen!

Debra Hamilton asserted, in her article "Top Ten Email Blunders that Cost Companies Money," that miscommunication cost even smaller companies of 100 employees an average of $420,000 per year.[3] That's a lot to lose simply because people aren't effectively communicating with each other.

Companies recognize the value of communication, which is why strong oral and written communication abilities are among the skills most sought by employers. For example, the *Job Outlook 2012* reported that the attributes employers prize the highest are "the ability to work in a team structure" (which is heavily dependent on effective communication) and the "ability to verbally communicate with persons inside and outside the organization."[4] These data were predicted by a 2010 American Management Association survey, which noted that over three-quarters of the respondents believed that communication skills would become more important over the next three to five years.[5]

So communication skills are essential, but you probably knew that. The critical problem—which you may also recognize—is that although worldwide surveys continue to confirm the importance of good communication, these same surveys consistently report that prospective and current employees are doing poorly enough to be labeled "deficient" in their communication skills.

IN ACTION

SHRM's professional HR Competency Model includes business acumen as the ninth and final competency. So much of the HR professional's success depends on "the ability to understand business functions and metrics within the organization and industry."[6] However, only effective communication skills enable HR professionals to make their business case. Even with all the HR knowledge in the world, practitioners' inability to communicate their understanding of the business will leave them unable to leverage their knowledge for the good of the organization.

The bottom line: HR professionals must be able to speak the language of business. Effective performance as a midlevel HR professional hinges on an ability to communicate the business case for HR initiatives.

Expert HR Communicators Needed!

Therefore, the HR practitioner with strong communication skills will be strategically positioned to have a great impact in the workplace. The role of HR professionals has become increasingly complex—and is likely to become even more complicated in the foreseeable future. Gone are the days of the personnel administrator sitting alone in a back office processing the company payroll, never to see the light of day or any real-life employees. Today's HR professionals have taken on a more strategic role that has increased their visibility throughout their organizations.

As strategic business partners, HR professionals interact with executives, line managers, rank-and-file employees, and outside stakeholders. With this increased visibility comes an opportunity to influence the organization and its strategic objectives. This opportunity, however, depends in large part on the HR professional's ability to effectively communicate up (to superiors), down (to subordinates), and sideways (to peers).

The 2012 Human Resource Competency Study led by Dave Ulrich and Wayne Brockbank identified six competencies required of HR professionals for success: being a credible activist, a strategic positioner, a champion for change, a technology proponent, an innovator and integrator, and a capability builder.[7]

Interestingly enough, these general competencies all require strong communication skills. The credible activist must be able to communicate well to build trusting relationships. As the strategic positioner, the HR professional must articulate to others the elements of the culture and its values, as well as the talent required for success. The change champion is responsible for initiating and supporting change, yet change is only successful when open, honest communication fuels the process. Effective communication is also essential in enabling the technology proponent to leverage new channels of communication to work for the business and contribute to the organization's success. In addition, one can be the most innovative person on the block, but without the skills to communicate ideas, those innovations are unlikely to be successfully integrated into healthy business practices. And finally, if HR professionals are entrusted to be capability builders, how else can they be successful but through thoughtful and strategic communication?

The message is clear in survey after survey: HR knowledge alone is not sufficient for success in the HR profession. In the *2008 Managing Your HR Career* survey report, 80 percent of HR professionals responding reported interpersonal communication as very important when advancing their careers.[8] Additionally, over 50 percent of HR professionals stated that interpersonal communication skills were among the top factors that helped them attain their current positions. And when asked what skills they thought were the most instrumental in landing that next job, interpersonal communication skills were again at the top of the list. Perhaps even more telling, directors and C-suite executives placed an even higher value on the need for interpersonal skills in the HR role: A total of 87 percent of directors and 83 percent of C-suite executives identified these skills as primary for success.[9]

This Book: A First Step toward Becoming More Valuable

HR professionals at all levels rely on strong communication skills to be successful in their roles. This book was written to help practitioners become better communicators, thereby making them better at their jobs and more valuable to their companies. In addition to general public and interpersonal speaking tips, the book specifically addresses the many hats of the HR professional. Whether in a generalist or specialist role, HR practitioners' wide range of responsibilities can only be effectively met with strong communication skills. Staffing the firm, training employees, developing and implementing policies, and integrating HR needs with the overall organization are all responsibilities that require effective communication.

The HR professional will need to become adept at speaking, which means channeling nervous energy into positive energy, presenting information logically, reading and using body language effectively, and supplementing verbal content with powerful visuals, all while seeming approachable and conversational. Chapter 2 offers tips and strategies to push you further in your general public speaking skills and provide you with new ways to approach that next event.

In addition to possessing general speaking skills, HR professionals must be competent communicators to succeed at one of their main tasks: workforce management. This function includes crafting a recruitment strategy, interviewing, welcoming new talent aboard, and then training and managing that new talent. Recruiting, selecting, and retaining talent require effective communication. Applicants will often forego employment with a company whose recruiter was not able to compellingly communicate what the position involved and specifics about the company.

HR development entails accurately training and deploying the workforce. This function has expanded into career planning as talent management has become a critical strategic challenge for organizations. As a helpful retention tool, HR professionals must be skilled in facilitating career discussions with the workforce, or else they risk losing key talent to a competitor.

The total rewards function of human resources encompasses all aspects of compensation and benefits. As more organizations outsource these functions, HR professionals find themselves managing these vendors and service providers in addition to their traditional workforce. The communication process has become more complex in this area as more international vendors are used, yet HR professionals must be savvy enough to manage these relationships with tact.

The employee and labor relations responsibility is also a communications function. Union bargaining agreements, grievances (both union and nonunion), and engagement programs are all, at their core, communication issues. During union negotiations, understanding the nuances of communication may mean the difference between gaining a concession and giving one up. Chapters 3 through 9 in this text discuss the key aspects of talent recruitment and management, from interviewing new hires to welcoming, training, and keeping them current on policies and procedures; they also discuss the delicate matters of delivering performance appraisals, handling problem employees, and maneuvering the termination interview. Any one of these tasks could be a landmine for the unprepared practitioner, and each situation has its own set of communication strategies.

DID YOU KNOW?

"Communication is a skill that you can learn. It's like riding a bicycle or typing. If you're willing to work at it, you can rapidly improve the quality of every part of your life."

– Brian Tracy

In addition to managing a company's talent, HR professionals need to be skilled communicators to relate their value to the organization's bottom line. This task requires the ability to gain buy-in from peers and superiors throughout the organization, and Chapters 10 and 11 offer strategies for creating collaborative environments with peers and managing up with superiors.

Additionally, special cases arise that require the unexpected. Some HR professionals may find themselves testifying in court, presenting information to regulatory agencies, or advising attorneys. Though they are not everyday occurrences, they are occasions that require careful communication and preparedness, topics covered in Chapter 12.

Finally, as key communicators in and for a company, HR professionals face opportunities each day to either increase or decrease their credibility. Chapter 13 highlights the mindset and readiness points needed to make each encounter a meaningful one.

Just as SHRM's professional HR Competency Model helps individuals "develop a road map to achieve your HR professional goals,"[10] this book draws on the application of those competencies to assist the HR professional in making a measurable impact on the organization's goals and outcomes.

With so much at stake in the HR arena today, HR professionals must be skilled communicators. In some cases, a failure to communicate successfully could land the company in court; in other cases, it could make the company unable to recruit and retain key talent; in all cases, it will cost the company money. By contrast, if we can better our communication skills, we can increase our value; that's what this book is all about.

Chapter 2

General Speaking Tips

As HR professionals, we know we'll need to do a lot of speaking to people, often in large groups, with the focus mostly on us. For some practitioners, this prospect fills them with fear and dread; for others, it inspires and energizes them; and for still others, it causes emotional shutdown and is viewed with a stoic nonchalance. We're here to tell you that fear is rational, and anxiety is normal.

The one common experience that all people have in response to the challenge of public speaking is adrenaline. Remember back to those biology classes when you learned about the fight or flight response that we have when faced with some kind of challenge? Physiologically, our bodies respond to public speaking with a fight or flight reaction. And the best thing our bodies have to fuel our fight or flight is adrenaline.

Adrenaline is what causes mouths to go dry, fingers to tremble, and voices to quiver. Our body feels a chemical overload that surges through our mind and muscles. The bad news is that we can't really control this reaction; however, the good news is that our body's response is meant for productivity, so we can use this physiological response proactively.

It's All Physiological!

Given that the adrenaline surge is a physical reaction, there are physical things we can do to manage and channel it. To be clear, the adrenaline surge we're talking about typically occurs close to the time of the presentation, so the practical tips we'll offer are things we can do just before and during a presentation.

First, because our body's chemical response is meant for action, moving is a great way to expend some of our excess energy. Going for a quick walk beforehand is one solution, and stretching is another. Each of these practical moves has physical implications for us. Walking allows some of that excess energy to flow out of our bodies. By engaging in some exercise before speaking, we can use up some of the adrenaline burst and begin the process of regulating our energy levels.

Walking also has a benefit similar to that of stretching: Both increase blood flow so that we are able to send the adrenaline all through our body and muscles instead of it having restricting flow. Stretching is even more productive, as it loosens up a wide range of muscles, creating greater blood flow throughout the body. If we take care to stretch our torso, arms, legs, and neck, we optimize blood flow, which in turn enables our body to more effectively act when it needs to do so.

Another common strategy to use before and during a presentation is controlled breathing. Taking steady, deep breaths furthers this idea of controlling our body's response to the adrenaline flood. Because we need oxygen for life processes, maximizing blood flow through exercise and stretching and optimizing oxygen intake through controlled breathing will regulate delivery of blood and oxygen to the brain.[1] That'll be important for us when it comes time for our brain to help us say things that make sense.

IN ACTION

SHRM's Competency Model identifies global and cultural effectiveness as "the art of managing human resources both within and across borders and cultures."[2] With the increasing diversity of nearly all workplaces, the creation of an inclusive organizational culture hinges on the actions of HR professionals.

Midlevel professionals are often tasked with developing and delivering diversity programs as well as resolving conflicts among organizational members as a result of differences in culture. Entry-level professionals need to demonstrate a "general awareness and understanding of cultural differences."[3]

So far, this advice should sound more like warming up for an athletic competition, and in fact, that's not a bad way to think about it. Speaking is a physical and mental event, just like a sporting event; therefore, our bodies must be well prepared. Likewise, the final piece of preparation to ensure our bodies are ready is to eat a healthy meal and get a good night's sleep before the event.

At this point, you might be thinking, "Eat a healthy meal and get sufficient sleep the night before? I am speaking in front of groups almost every day!" We're glad you brought this up. The point is that, to some extent, becoming a good speaker and managing the anxiety that comes with public speaking is a lifestyle. If we are consistently speaking in front of others, then we need to be consistently taking measures to ensure our bodies are ready for the challenge.

But of course, just as every good athlete knows that playing a game well is about more than just physical readiness, you also know that delivering a great presentation is about more than just a brisk walk and a good stretching routine before facing the crowd. We can also prepare mentally to effectively manage our nervous energy.

This advice is not revolutionary, but it bears repeating: When mentally managing anxiety before and during a speech performance, nothing beats practicing. Athletes know this; musicians know this; the military knows this. It is the reason a concert violinist will repeat a single run hundreds of times in practice or an Army Ranger will practice cleaning a rifle blindfolded: When the pressure is on, they want to be able to do it instinctively.

The kind of practice we do is extremely important. As in the examples of the violinist and the Ranger, we too must physically practice if we hope to perform well under pressure. When we actually speak our presentations aloud over and over, beginning to end, we essentially create a neurological path in our brain. Just as if you were to walk around and around on the same area of your lawn, it would make a rut, when we practice the speech over and over again, we wear a rut in our brains. When we give the presentation, our mind will know all the words we want to speak because that pathway is there. Nothing soothes nerves like knowing we are well prepared.

Now that we've discussed the physiological responses to the challenge of public speaking, permit us a philosophical moment: Fear comes when there is a threat—real or perceived—to something we care about. In public speaking, we often feel fear because we realize that our performance affects our reputation and other people's lives—two things that we should care about. People may try to tell themselves they're not worried about their public speaking events, but if they care about their reputation and about their audiences (making good use of their time, giving them accurate information, and helping them in some way), then they should feel some butterflies about whether or not they are going to accomplish such meaningful tasks.

The key is that by identifying some of the common causes of the fear, we can minimize its effects. If we feel fear because we care about our audience members, we will take care not to waste their time, offer incomplete information, or give them useless ideas; therefore, we will feel more confident about our presentation. If our presentations are relevant, engaging, and helpful, people will be more likely to value our contributions, thus safeguarding our reputations.

It's a Generation Thing…Try to Understand

And now for some practical advice about examining our audience. Most of our presentations fall somewhere along a spectrum that has two poles: information that must be delivered and information we want people to get excited about, meaning that our presentations fall somewhere between informational and persuasive, with plenty of overlaps. When we are training employees or teaching them the ropes of a new system or policy, we're in an informational mode, but when we're trying to secure buy-in from peers or bosses on an idea, we are in a persuasive mode. The main determinant as to the effectiveness of either of these attempts is how well we match our message to our audience.

Thoroughly examining our audience enables us to know what to say and how to say it. Knowing what to say is about knowing what makes our audiences tick—the things they care about and are invested in. Knowing how to say it is about knowing the communication style they will respond to best.

Examining audiences to know what to say involves thinking about their values, which are directly related to their demographics. People of different genders, cultures, personalities, levels of ability, age brackets, and socioeconomic groups value different things, and often, we are faced with demographically varied audiences. To appeal to multiple groups at the same time, we need to find common denominators. Some of the most common things people care about are their money, time, family, career, well-being, and relationships; however, the complicated part is that different groups have distinct approaches to each of these. The best speakers strategically position their messages to touch on the values of the maximum number of people in their audience. When we can show audiences that we are helping them regarding some of these values, they are more likely to pay attention to our information.

Knowing how to talk to our audiences requires our understanding the kinds of communication styles audiences prefer. Some groups like PowerPoint, whereas others want flip charts, and still others favor conversation. As well, different groups prefer different levels of formality or background knowledge.

Perhaps the best overall guideline to address diverse groups is to adhere to the "Titanium Rule" proposed by Dr. Susan Murphy: "Do unto others, keeping their preferences in mind."[4] Her principle means that, instead of communicating in the way that meets our needs, we will be better served by adjusting to others and their needs. We can identify some clues to their styles and preferences by simply observing their experiences and values.

Four generations now occupy the workplace—and soon there will be five! The Silent Generation (also referred to as the Traditionalists and Veterans) is the oldest of the four. Though mostly retired now, they comprise people born between 1922 and 1945. They were most influenced by the Great Depression.

The widely researched Baby Boomers are people born between 1946 and 1964. Their sheer size (78 million strong) and world events such as the war in Vietnam and the assassinations of President John F. Kennedy and Rev. Martin Luther King Jr. shaped their development. Having grown up in an age of prosperity and social upheaval, they are focused on changing the world. Woodstock lives on in these workaholics! However, as this generation prepares for retirement in record numbers, many HR professionals and top-level managers worry that their institutional knowledge has not been well managed and passed on.

Members of Generation X (also simply called Xers) were born roughly between 1965 and 1979. They have also been referred to as the Baby Bust generation, reflecting the small size of this generation. This was the first generation of latchkey kids (due to working moms), which explains their incredible independence. They may also be leery of organizational loyalty because they saw their parents laid off by corporate America in record numbers.

The latest generation to enter the workforce is referred to as Millennials (also Nexters or Generation Y or Gen Y). They were born between 1980 and 1995 (some experts have said they reach as far as 2002). In addition to their helicopter parents, perhaps their greatest characteristic is their comfort with and focus on technology. They don't know a world without technology! And their parents have created a generation in which many feel "special" and expect to be treated as such. The Millennial generation values diversity, workplace flexibility, and social responsibility.

With this information in mind, we might consider how a diverse audience would perceive us as speakers—particularly with different generations in attendance. If we are from the Silent generation, we might assess whether we are too rigid and appear to lack openness to new ideas. Using technology—especially with Millennials who have grown up with technology—will help bridge some generational gaps. Those of us Baby Boomers might consider whether we appear too serious, "corporate," or "buttoned up." If we are members of Generation X, we might assess whether we sometimes appear too casual or independent. And we Millennials might consider if we sometimes come across as impatient, unfocused, or even naive.

When speaking to an audience composed of multiple generations, using a wide range of examples will help people from the different generations relate.

A-Okay Is Not Okay in Some Cultures

Just as knowing our audiences means thinking through some of their generational preferences, it also means examining their cultural and ethnic composition. Although the United States was once described as a melting pot, this analogy no longer seems to reflect today's workforce. Harriet Hankin described the workforce as a mosaic,[5] and more recent descriptions have used the analogies of a symphony, a salad, or a stew. All of these suggest that we want individuals to maintain their uniqueness while mixing in well with others.

Part of communicating more effectively with a diverse audience is beginning to understand our own biases and how our experiences and values shape the lens through which we view our world. We cannot assume that others share our view of the world. This misassumption creates a disconnect between us and our audience, and it can sometimes be seen as ethnocentric. We need to study our audiences and inspect our words and gestures carefully to ensure nothing in our presentation suggests that we assume our way is superior to how another culture might operate.

DID YOU KNOW?

Aristotle argued that what makes humans distinct is our hearts, minds, and souls; therefore, if we want to connect with a crowd, we must appeal to all these levels. We need to show our audiences how our information is logically beneficial, emotionally satisfying, and ethically sound.

Below are some tips to follow when communicating with diverse audiences:

- *Eliminate figurative language.* Phrases such as, "Now the shoe's on the other foot" or "Let's hit this one out of the park," are everyday statements that we use without noticing them, but these phrases may at best confuse audiences from other cultures.
- *Remember that nonverbal communication is critical.* Our nonverbal component may reinforce, contradict, or even substitute for our verbal communication, so we must study these cultural differences ahead of time. For example, forming an "O" with our thumb and forefinger, which for people in the United States means "a-okay," "perfect," or "got it," is an obscenity in some cultures, carrying much different meanings.
- *Keep your presentation straightforward and brief.* The more we talk, the more we will regress to our own dialect and habits, so we should plan exactly what we need to say and how we need to say it and then do so directly.
- *Ask questions and rephrase comments.* Checking in with audiences is a good habit and is particularly useful with multicultural audiences. As well, rephrasing comments or questions when audience members give feedback will ensure we understand them well.
- *Research linguistic preferences.* Just as knowing nonverbal signs and their meanings benefits us, we also need to know different cultures' verbal tendencies. For example, in some cultures, the preferred pronoun is "she," whereas in others, it is "he;" still other cultures vary pronoun usage or use "they" when possible to avoid gender preferences.

Perhaps the bottom line is that we want to offer something to everyone in our audience. Our goal should be to create an inclusive environment. Once we have determined our audience's preferences with regard to values and style, crafting a presentation they will find helpful and relevant becomes much easier.

Let's Get Visual

The next decision—which must also be made in light of our audience's preferences—is what, if any, visual aids will be used to supplement the talk. Because such a wide range of visual aids is available to speakers—from presentation software such as PowerPoint and Prezi to flip charts to magic tricks—we have many decisions to make when we choose to use one of them. Two guiding questions we can ask ourselves are "How will my visual further my point?" and "What's the risk/reward ratio?"

The first question to consider is how the visual aid will supplement our message and enable more audience members to remember and apply what we have spoken about. In their article in *Educational Psychologist*, Mayer and Moreno pointed out that we learn through both verbal and visual channels, but speakers may overload their audience's verbal channels during a presentation, since that's the channel that is already processing information.[6]

If a speaker relies on a visual aid that is primarily textual, then the audience is forced to both read and listen, which often results in verbal channel overload: People either stop listening or stop reading because they realize that when they try to do both, they miss things. The best way, then, to augment our message with a visual aid is to actually make it visual. Thus, our job is to figure out what visuals will best complement our words. For example, organizing numbers graphically shows audiences what the numbers physically look like in the context of other numbers.

People remember better through repetition; however, listening to a speaker simply saying the same words over and over again gets pretty boring. Pictures provide another means of repetition, but because they access a different channel for processing information, audience members receive a set of information through both their verbal and visual channels. This method maximizes their potential recall ability.

Our first job is to decide how to most productively repeat our message pictographically. Our second job is to recognize that every visual aid comes with potential risks and potential rewards, and examining what we stand to lose or gain from a particular visual is time well spent. For instance,

DID YOU KNOW?

When addressing audiences composed of individuals who speak English as a second language, speaking more slowly may aid in successful transfer of information. Avoid the tendency to speak louder.

single-sheet handouts may be easily posted on people's office walls, but they can also distract audience members if they are reading through the handout while listening to us. PowerPoint presentations may be visually engaging (when done properly), but as printouts, they may be clunky. Flip-charts may encourage audience interaction, but they may also be hard to read or seem too old-fashioned. Thinking through our audience's needs and preferences can help us select the visual aid that will be most productive for them.

Use What Your Momma Gave You

Even if we decide against a formal visual aid, we still have at least two innate presentation aids: our voices and our bodies. These are our natural tools to supplement the content we're delivering, so we need to use them effectively.

It's certainly true that we need to make sure we speak loudly enough for everyone to hear; however, most of our vocal chords have a wide range of capabilities, and the most interesting speakers recognize this range and use it to their advantage. If we want audiences to have the best chance of paying attention over a longish period of time, we should vary the rate, tone, and volume with which we talk. For example, nothing can cause an audience to sit forward and listen like a speaker dropping his or her voice down to a whisper. As well, changing the rate at which we talk may increase audience attentiveness too. The normal rule of thumb is to maintain a relatively slow rate of speaking, but speeding up for a time may be a useful tactic to emphasize an aspect of the presentation.

When using our bodies to effectively enhance our presentations, the primary thing we can do is to be active. Moving around up front helps audiences pay attention because it requires them to physically move a little to watch us—their eyes follow us, and their heads move at times to keep up.

In addition to being physically active, we also want our bodies to portray activity or energy. Therefore, actions like keeping both hands in our pockets or fiddling with jewelry are off limits because they seem like passive and withdrawn kinds of movements. The same goes for standing behind a podium for too long: It eventually starts to seem as if the presenter is hiding instead of actively engaging his or her audience.

In closing, two parting shots: First, place special emphasis on your transitions, and second, go to the trouble of creating a captivating introduction to your presentation. Transitions are the lifelines that audience members use to reorient themselves if they zone out for a minute. Let's face it—people zone in and out periodically throughout presentations, so using clear, obvious transitions that remind folks of where we just were and where we are headed next may be the difference between people zoning out and staying out or their feeling that they actually remember most of what we talked about.

Finally, sometimes we find ourselves giving talks to the same basic groups of people, so we may not feel the need to establish rapport with them or to ease them into a topic. The temptation in these instances is not to perform at the same level of quality as we would for the presentations with higher stakes. Nonetheless, audiences appreciate when we still work to please them, and adding some pre-speech entertainment never hurts. Taking the time to add some spice to the beginning of our presentations may make us one of the few folks in our company people actually look forward to listening to.

Chapter 3

Orientation Programs: The Welcome Speech

Some newly hired employees will stride into their orientation meetings with poise and confidence, whereas others will face the situation with anxious inexperience. Still others may act defensively or bored, trying to communicate that they're highly skilled at the job they've come to do.

Regardless of their demeanors, all of them need a sense of acceptance and belonging. This means that it's up to us to create that kind of environment. Given the variety of personalities and attitudes in a workplace, attempting to make everyone feel comfortable and part of a team is a challenge.

Because every organization will have a different level of content that must be delivered in its orientation program, this chapter will not focus on how to communicate information (Chapters 2, 4, and 5 contain those kinds of tips); instead, it will focus on creating a sense of inclusiveness and team spirit among newly-recruited employees and current employees.

The main things to remember during an orientation session are to maintain a high level of enthusiasm, a lively pace of activity, and a positive, encouraging tone. These general principles will help keep our audiences engaged, prevent them from becoming bored or overwhelmed by the material, and help them feel excited about the new relationship they are beginning with our company.

Energy: Fake It 'Til You Make It?

A high level of enthusiasm is pretty difficult to fake. Therefore, if we are going to be exciting speakers, we actually need to be excited. So...how do you feel about the company you're working for? How well do you like your job? Are you enthusiastic about welcoming new talent into your company? If positive thoughts came to mind as you read those questions, you will have a much easier time conveying authentic energy. If not, there are ways to "fake" emotion and positivity, and sometimes performing or acting out a role can, over time, become something we enjoy.

Some of the concrete ways we can evince enthusiasm are through our voice and body language. We'll focus on voice when we discuss principles for maintaining a positive and encouraging tone. A speaker's body language communicates enthusiasm through the face, hands, and general movement of the speaker.

People call the eyes a portal to the soul because they have the potential to convey so much about a person. People who do not maintain eye contact are considered untrustworthy; rapid blinkers are considered nervous; and wide-eyed people are considered innocent—the list can go on. During a presentation, a speaker's eyes are part of the overall facial expression that helps communicate enthusiasm to an audience. Opening our eyes wider raises our eyebrows and makes our whole face light up and seem more energetic and interested. This is a simple, general move we can make to consistently convey excitement through our eyes.

IN ACTION

The relationship management competency is at the heart of the HR professional's role as a strategic business partner.[1] Managing relationships and building credibility begin on day one with orientation. Our role of introducing new people into the company reinforces a relationship of mutual respect fostered by human resources throughout the organization, and it promotes a culture of openness and approachability. Thus, orientations enable all organizational members to see—and experience—human resources' service role.

We can also use our eyes to make everyone in the audience feel included. Looking at one person or group of people may make others feel excluded, but looking throughout the entire audience and giving approximately the same amount of eye contact to each quadrant of a room enables each person to know that the speaker feels he or she is important. Speakers naturally tend to look more at the people in the audience they want to impress. Sometimes it's a boss, but it can just as easily be a favored or more experienced colleague. If we aren't careful, we run the risk of alienating some audience members who feel excluded by our lack of eye contact.

A related practical tip is that left-handed people tend to look more to their right and right-handed people tend to look more to their left. Knowing this information may help us scan the room more effectively.

Additionally, we can use our eyes to supplement the content of our speeches as we tell stories or communicate major details. For instance, closing your eyes and raising your eyebrows can playfully say, "I'm not listening," or furrowing your eyebrows and squinting or narrowing your eyes can help you say, "I find this suspicious—how about you?" Strategically using our eyes can help us energize our speeches and keep our audiences aroused.

Our eyes can also help us display friendly and open facial expressions that enable our audiences to connect with us. Audiences confirm that they enjoy speakers who look approachable and kind, qualities often conveyed when speakers smile genuinely and make comfortable eye contact. As well, our facial expressions need to match the tone and emotion of our speech content. Our faces should carry the expression we hope our audience members will wear on their faces: bright interest.

Hand movement is another tool speakers use to display enthusiasm. A speaker whose hands remain locked onto the podium is unlikely to generate a sense of urgency, excitement, or engagement, compared to one whose hands are out and appropriately accentuating the details of the speech. The key, of course, is to augment our speeches with *appropriate* gestures.

Some simple examples of appropriate gestures are numbering points with our fingers, using our arms to enact portions of stories or measurements of distance, and moving in expected ways to complement common phrases (for example, shrugging your shoulders to go along with "I don't know"). The general rule of thumb is to use gestures you would normally use in everyday life. Some people use their hands more than others when they talk, so there is some level of personality at play here; however, we must avoid either using our hands so much that they overtake the presentation or using them in repetitive ways that become as noticeable and distracting as a verbal tic such as "uh" or "um." (Consider, hypothetically, the speaker who sporadically raises her right hand away from her side throughout her speech—do it a handful of times while speaking to yourself in the mirror and you'll see how distracting this can be.)

Finally, moving around the room also helps communicate our enthusiasm and energy to audiences because they can actually *see* our enthusiasm coming out through our bodies. A bit of movement also helps keep the audience engaged. If we stand still, audience members' eyes stare at one spot, without any variety, causing them to tire, lose focus, or become dis-interested. When we move around the room, our audience follows with their eyes and heads, sometimes even with their bodies, keeping them physically involved and possibly contributing to greater mental involvement as well.

Moving around the room well requires knowing the room so as not to trip over or bump into things. It also requires that we move in a smooth, unobtrusive way. If we walk too quickly back and forth over a small stretch of carpet, we may look like a pacing tiger; however, if we move in somewhat random patterns across the front of the room or around it, we will achieve our goal of looking casual and composed. Audiences often interpret standing still as passive, so if we move throughout the room, it will enable them to feel more connected with us.

Pick Up the Pace—And Keep It Up!

In addition to having lively body language, we should also keep up a lively pace with the content we deliver. We don't need to change topics every 15 minutes; granted, some topics need an hour's worth of discussion. However, when covering longer topics, varying our delivery style will help keep the audience's attention. For instance, perhaps one portion may be discussed in a Q&A format, another using PowerPoint, and another using physical props. Breaking the information delivery into smaller segments will keep things energetic and upbeat—for our audience and for us.

Breaking the information into smaller segments will assist in audience recall and prevent audience members from feeling overwhelmed. A presenter who is giving an hour-long explanation of his or her company's benefits program might begin with physical props, move to a Q&A format in which audience members first divide into groups and discuss the questions they would like to have answered, and then end with a PowerPoint that graphically displays the relevant information. This kind of presentation has the potential to mildly entertain, while encouraging connection among new employees. It would also potentially result in greater recall of information for audience members because they saw objects and pictures that reinforced the information, and they talked among themselves about particular aspects of the information.

Positivity: It's, Like, Super-Duper Important! (Seriously Though—It Is)

When we strive to welcome new people during an orientation session, our creativity is often our greatest asset in developing small presentation segments that engage participants and make them feel a sense of positivity about their new place of employment.

Positivity is also communicated through how we speak, which encompasses what we say and how we say it. Like enthusiasm, making sure what we say is positive and upbeat is hard to fake. If you dislike your company, using words and terms that display your company in a positive light will be difficult. Fake positivity in language often causes speakers to go overboard with their adverbs and adjectives, which tends to make audiences skeptical (of the benefits, co-workers, and bosses that are "really pretty outstandingly super-amazing").

In other words, we have to take care that our language is balanced and realistic, yet firmly optimistic and encouraging. One simple way to start off with encouraging language is to use "we" as often as it fits. For example, look back at the opening sentence of this paragraph (as well as the entire book); where appropriate, "we" is used to not sound like an overlord talking down to an underling ("I" and "you") but rather like two teammates talking to each other on a level field ("we" and "us"). It's a small word, but it has great power to encourage unity.

We have many practical ways to use language positively and to encourage inclusiveness, but most of them are situation-specific. In general, using positive language takes conscious practice, and speakers may benefit from mentally walking through the planned phrases and comments to make during a welcome session or speech; we can also videotape ourselves for analysis.

For example, as you analyze your language, consider how your tone might change if the CEO of the company were sitting in on your orientation. A statement such as, "It takes forever to get reimbursements, so if you want to get mileage reimbursement for a business trip, you'd better submit your forms as soon as humanly possible," might become, "If you go on a business trip and need mileage reimbursement, you'll want to start the paperwork as soon as you get back because the process takes about two weeks."

Notice in the example that positive language usage often means switching around how we begin our sentences because the order affects the main focus of the sentence. In the first sentence, the focus is on how long the process takes, whereas in the second example, the focus is on business trips and on some of the considerations that come along with them. Upbeat speakers don't focus on the negatives; instead, they focus on productivity and actions.

Additionally, notice that the first sentence inserts a value judgment about the process: "It takes forever." The second sentence refrains from judgment and simply reports the facts: "The process takes about two weeks." The principle here is the same one our mothers taught us when we were young—"If you can't say something nice, don't say anything at all."

Taking some time to think about *what* we say can help us ensure that our message is welcoming and that it encourages unity. Taking some time to analyze *how* we say things can also help us in this endeavor. Analyzing how we say things comes down to thinking about how we can use our voices enthusiastically.

Enthusiasm in our voices may come from our vocal volume and pace—as discussed in Chapter 2. But we also need tonal variety to keep our voices interesting. For instance, it's tonal variety that

DID YOU KNOW?...

You might play with that volume button a little. To command attention, try dropping your voice to a lower volume. Though whispering may seem counterintuitive, shouting at an audience gets old. Varying volume may also signal a transition, which can perk up audience attention.

makes a good storyteller, but identifying tonal idiosyncrasies in our own voices is often difficult. Listening to ourselves talk can help with this, but videotaping ourselves will be the most promising means of rating our speaking tones.

The most easily identified issue is monotone, but we need to recognize other distracting patterns too. Often, speakers fall into sing-song tones or have incorporated "up-talking" tendencies without realizing it. ("Up-talking" is when speakers end each sentence as if it were a question—try it with the sentences in this paragraph and you'll hear how funny it sounds.) Listening to ourselves can help us hear oddities or distracting tonal patterns. The goal is to sound conversational instead of staged, forced, or overdone.

The principles of enthusiasm, an active pace, and positivity are generalities that may help welcome new employees and enable them to feel excited about becoming part of a new team. There are also more specific ways to plan ahead and build a welcoming experience for them. Below, we offer practical ideas for icebreakers and team-building exercises, ways to create connections between new and current employees, and techniques for fostering fun and inclusive conversations. We also discuss the importance of allowing some personal downtime for the new hires.

Let's Break That Ice

Icebreakers and team-building exercises provide informal and unique opportunities for participants to get to know each other on a different level than normal work experiences. These are the kinds of connections that will last beyond just the knowledge that two people both happen to be accountants (which, let's be honest, probably isn't that exciting).

To be inclusive, we must always evaluate the exercises we have planned in light of the participants. For instance, one idea discussed below is a scavenger hunt; our responsibility is to make sure that we have an adequately accessible facility or that the hunt is limited enough in range that everyone will be able to enjoy the activity. Having a few backup plans is also a good idea, just to be sure we will be able to introduce activities that enable everyone to connect.

The Famous Duos game may function as a stand-alone ice breaker or as a two-part exercise to break the ice and then transition into group introductions. To prepare, we will need to brainstorm some fun, famous couples or search online for "famous couples." Some good examples are Superman and Lois Lane, Bill and Hillary Clinton, and peanut butter and jelly. The key is to choose well-known duos so that participants won't feel silly for not recognizing the names. Once we have our list of famous duos, we write each individual name on a nametag.

To begin the game, place a nametag on the back of each person, but be sure the person does not see the name. The goal of the game is for each person to find his or her partner, and the one rule is that people cannot simply ask, "Hey, what does my nametag say?" Participants need to cooperate with others by asking for clues about their own identity and by offering clues about the identities of others.

Rules for the actual conversations are up to the person running the show. One idea is to only allow people to ask "yes" or "no" questions, such as, "Am I imaginary?" or "Am I in show business?" Another idea is to limit people to one question per encounter to encourage maximum interaction throughout the group.

The game ends when all the partners have found each other; however, we can foster further conversation by adding a second element to the game. Having the duos introduce each other to the group at the end of the activity will motivate more probing conversation. Specific introduction criteria may be offered, or people can just find out what they want to about each other. Either way, participants will have a greater opportunity to learn more about each other.

The next icebreaker idea is called People Bingo, and it can be general or customized to a specific group of people if you know something about them or if they have submitted specific information ahead of time. To create the bingo card, set up a 25 cell table in your word processing system of choice (for example, Word, Excel, Pages, Numbers). In each cell, write a characteristic such as, "Runs Marathons," "Loves Chocolate," or "Only Child." If you solicited specific information ahead of time, you can pick out some fun, little-known facts, but if not, you can devise more general ones.

Once all the bingo cards are handed out, participants walk around and ask questions to get to know each other. When they find someone who has a characteristic listed on the bingo chart, they write that person's name in the box. The first person to get five boxes in a row yells "Bingo!" and reads his or her five in a row for confirmation. This is another game that encourages conversation among group members and helps them learn more about each other than they would in a normal workday encounter.

Finally, a scavenger hunt brings an even more physically active approach to team-building exercises because it gets people up and walking around the building. Though it could be a little less personally interactive, a scavenger hunt has the added potential of familiarizing new hires with the company facilities, and we assume they would have at least some conversation while they hunted. The list of items may be customized to bring the new members into contact with crucial departments and people throughout the organization, provided the people affected know ahead of time that their workday may be briefly interrupted.

As with everything else about the welcoming process, the hope is that icebreakers and team-building activities provide active, engaging ways for people to begin to connect with each other and with their new place of employment. Some orientations might—of necessity—be full of sitting and listening, but exercises like these are important to include so that the newcomers have a chance to stretch their legs and enjoy each other.

Newbie, Meet Veteran; Veteran, Newbie

If one of the main priorities of an orientation program is to help the newly hired employees feel like part of the team, then we not only have to connect them with each other, but we also have to connect them with current team members. In other words, we need to intentionally set up ways to build bonds between the new folks and the seasoned folks. This process may take a variety of forms, depending on the orientation agenda and the culture of our company. Involving some of the current employees in icebreakers and team-building exercises and inviting some of them to lunch, an idea discussed below, are a few easy options.

Regardless of how we plan to introduce the new team members to current employees, it's our job to help achieve meaningful connections instead of awkward encounters. There are two basic avenues for potential connections—work expertise and personal interests; planning ahead will help us suc-

DID YOU KNOW?

Humor can help us deliver our message, as long as it's appropriate. Jeff Davidson, in *The Complete Guide to Public Speaking*, suggests that we first get a read on the "humor level" of our audience members. They will tend to listen more if they are smiling and enjoying themselves.[3]

cessfully connect new and experienced personnel.

The first step is finding current employees who enjoy their job and are interested in welcoming new employees. There is no surer recipe for unproductive meetings than pairing newcomers with veterans who either are not fond of the company or have been coerced into being part of the orientation process. The cheerful, friendly faces at our company are gems when welcoming new folks on board.

Additionally, we recommend gathering a group of veterans from a variety of walks of life and areas of expertise so that we have a greater potential for matching people up well. After polling the incoming employees ahead of time, we can then pair them with the welcomer who best matches their interests.

Some companies use personality profiling methods to get to know their employees and potential hires, which can be a great resource for collecting information about people's skills and interests. Regardless of whether our company has this kind of system, we need to collect data about the team of welcomers and the new hires. If we know about the veteran and the newcomer, the introduction shifts from, "John, this is Jane from payroll—you'll be working with her," to "John, this is Jane, who works in your department. She's a mountain biker, just like you." This opening provides John and Jane with an initial point of conversation and saves them from having to search for it themselves.

Lunch, Anyone?

Some orientation sessions span a full day or more and therefore include a lunch hour. Instead of leaving the new employees to fend for themselves, lunch offers another prime moment for connection. Some folks might feel awkward having to find lunch-mates and initiate their own conversations, so if we prepare ahead of time, we can turn the lunch hour into another opportunity to form bonds in the company.

Having something enjoyable to do during the lunch hour is often a good plan; however, the time does not need to be formal and scheduled. We may have an officially communicated activity for people to do while they lunch, or we might simply suggest some interesting questions to ask each other to spur conversation within the group.

If we have a small group of people who can all sit comfortably around a table and hear one another talk, we may want to be the informal emcee of the lunch. We would then come prepared with questions that will draw people out to get everyone participating and learning about each other. However, when we have a large group that requires several tables to accommodate, we can give each table the same basic questions by writing them on separate pieces of paper and placing them in a bowl on the table. Each newcomer chooses a piece of paper and then they all take turns chatting about the questions.

Sample questions are listed below:
- What's your favorite story from high school? (or college, if we're sure everyone has attended college)
- What personal achievement are you most proud of?
- What was your best vacation?
- What would you name as the most interesting fact about yourself?

A few principles should guide your choice of questions. First, the questions need to be accessible to everyone, which, for instance, is why you might confine the first question to high school, unless you were certain that everyone attended college. Nothing blocks connection like asking a question that excludes people. For example, imagine lunching with a bunch of rich executives, and one of them says, "I know—let's go around the table and all tell where our vacation homes are located!" Um, the hammock in my backyard?

Additionally, the questions should help people learn about each other, but they should not be so personal as to be uncomfortable. It's true that someone's answer to the second question may be, "Toilet-papering my ex-boss' car last week," but in general, we hope that our interview process was savvy enough to eliminate the folks who might offer inappropriate information about themselves. Asking questions that help the group learn about each other will deepen their connection with each other and, by extension, with the company.

Finally, the questions should promote fun discussion. Although our hope is that everyone answers the questions, our ultimate goal is simply to get everyone participating and talking so that the lunch hour is not another strain on our new hires but rather a relaxing and enjoyable break.

Not Everyone's an Extrovert

As much as we hope that a pleasant group discussion over lunch will offer an enjoyable break for the newcomers, we have to acknowledge that not everyone is an extrovert, so not everyone will find the encounter relaxing. Some people will have a great time with the icebreakers, group discussions, and lunchtime chat, but other people may be exhausted from not having any downtime to take a breath on their own.

Therefore, we may want to consciously build in some short periods of alone time throughout the day. These can be a few 15 to 20 minute breaks that offer folks unstructured time to chat informally, head out to their car to read a book, or do whatever other personal activity that recharges them.

Whatever the specifics of our orientation sessions, the main goal is not just to familiarize the incoming employees with the company; it's also to create a stronger sense of connection and team spirit between them and the company. We can foster this bond through our energetic and inclusive presentations and activities.

Chapter 4

Training Sessions

There are tons of trainers out there today. There are cross trainers, personal trainers, dog trainers. There's spring training, basic training, strength training. There are training wheels, training collars, training bras. They all promise training, but the kind of training they deliver varies dramatically. Our goal in this chapter is to outline how to run dynamic and memorable training sessions that achieve a high transfer of information.

Training is provided to assist individual learners (and the organization) in meeting their goals. It may benefit the organization by helping to improve employee motivation, enhance employee performance, and achieve company goals.

Those organizations that make the strategic choice to "make" their employees (versus "buy" them) rely heavily on training to ensure that the employees develop the appropriate skill set. But even for the organizations that choose to "buy" their employees, skill sets must be constantly updated to keep employees current and to develop individuals for future opportunities. Therefore, a systematic approach to training is essential to increase the probability of a greater return on investment of those training dollars.

The Systematic Approach to Training

The systematic approach to training involves four phases: needs assessment, training design, delivery, and evaluation. During the needs assessment phase, an analysis is conducted on three levels to identify training needs: organizational, task, and person. The analysis asks, "What are the training needs for our entire organization, for specific tasks performed within our organization, and for specific people within our organization?" For example, if a new software program is going to be introduced to the marketing department, a strategic needs assessment would recognize training needs on a task level for that department. If, however, a group of people scored poorly on customer service after the last round of performance evaluations, a needs assessment would identify training opportunities on a people level.

Identifying the training needs is critical because realizing a favorable return on our investment necessitates our spending money on areas of need: If we offer training on subjects our people already excel in, we waste their time and our training dollars.

IN ACTION

SHRM's consultation competency involves "the art of providing direct guidance to organizational stakeholders...seeking expert advice on a variety of situations or circumstances."[1] This excerpt speaks directly to the ability of human resources to provide training, development, and coaching opportunities to the workforce at all organizational levels. The key is to provide business solutions to drive the strategy of the organization. Training and development programs address this challenge directly.

Needs assessment also guides the training design, delivery, and evaluation phases. Once we have identified which needs most deserve training dollars, we can then move on to constructing an appropriate system of training, with objectives that identify what we want participants to know or to be able to do once they complete the training. These objectives then help determine what kind of delivery style will be most effective. Finally, the evaluation process follows up on the initial objectives to determine if they were actually met.

We will focus this chapter primarily on the delivery of the training, since this is a communication book; however, any good teacher knows that good delivery of material is meaningless if the material is not relevant to the audience. For this reason, we highlight the importance of identifying areas of need, generating clear objectives based on those needs, and following up with an evaluation to determine the effectiveness of the training.

What Method Will Guide Our Madness?

Once we have performed a needs assessment and identified concrete objectives for our training, we can turn to the act of designing and delivering the presentation. Training objectives should fuel the design and delivery of the presentation.

Some delivery approaches better suit our needs than others. For example, if our objective is to make our employees more aware of the new chain of command and how and why it works, our presentation style will probably consist of lecture and discussion. If our objective is to help people be more cordial on the telephone, our presentation style will probably incorporate more experiential methods such as simulations and role playing, along with some lecture and discussion.

Although many trainers choose lecture as their default mode, that's not always the best choice. Especially when large amounts of information need to be transferred, lectures may drone on for too long and be too complicated. And as noted in Chapter 2, we should tune our style to the generational and cultural demographics of our audience. If we need to pass along a lot of information, text is often a better method. Providing text allows trainees to process the material in their own time and at their own speed, and then we have the opportunity to run a discussion session at a later date and offer any necessary clarifications.

Just as people learn in different ways, they also remember information best when they are given multiple angles on the material. As we train employees, then, our goal should be to engage them in as many different avenues of learning as possible. Employees should have the opportunity to listen to us talk about the material, discuss the material with co-workers, see visuals related to the material, and when appropriate, actually practice what they're learning.

To BE Spectacular, We've Got to Plan for It

Pulling off a successful training session doesn't come from luck; it comes from preparation. It has been said that spectacular achievements come from unspectacular preparation. If we are not prepared or are lacking in subject-area expertise, the audience can tell immediately! Preparing for the training session by studying the material and practicing the presentation will boost our self-confidence. Audiences read both of these things almost instantaneously and decide whether we have credibility or not. When we feel competent internally and seem competent externally to our audience, we will deliver more effective and transformative training.

To prepare for our audience, we might send a questionnaire to them in advance, asking what they expect to gain from the session and confirming their attendance. Questionnaires can also help us gauge our audience's knowledge and skill level so that we can better define our training objectives. Knowing our audience—who we'll be speaking to, as well as their expectations—will enable us to better meet their expectations and our learning objectives.

On the day of the training session, arriving at least 30 minutes early will allow us time to check the setup of the room, test any equipment, confirm that session materials are on hand, and be ready to greet the participants as they arrive. This habit of arriving early will prove invaluable for ironing out last-minute glitches that often occur and can be avoided through good preparation.

Arriving early also gives us time to interact with audience members and get to know their names and faces before the presentation begins so that we can continue to build rapport with them throughout the session. This will help us connect with our audience, thereby enabling them to learn better. This kind of unspectacular preparation lays the foundation for a spectacular performance.

You Teach Your Mother in That Room?

A spectacular training performance means that we have both entertained the audience and educated them in a lasting way so that they will remember and implement the material in the days and weeks to come. A key to achieving this goal is creating an environment where learning feels natural and easy, and some of the choices we make ahead of time influence the kind of learning environment we construct. Specifically, the room we select will contribute to how easily the audience learns.

The shape of the room is important. For example, learning is more difficult in long, narrow rooms where listeners seated in the back will have difficulty seeing, hearing, and paying attention. (Incidentally, this configuration describes most conference rooms. Although sitting around a table may foster brainstorming, the layout inhibits training sessions if participants cannot see or hear well. Additionally, conference rooms often prevent presenters from moving easily around the room.)

Often, square-shaped rooms are more effective because the seating can be arranged and rearranged to accommodate different training styles and activities. Attention to the layout of the chairs can enhance communication or erect barriers. A semicircular seating arrangement lends itself to easy interaction between participants because everyone can see each other's faces. Classroom seating, on the other hand, is often used for more traditional lectures without much group work.

Another room consideration is the size. Using a room with a capacity for 500 people to accommodate a group of 50 may create an impersonal environment because of our distance from the participants and their possible distance from each other.

Inspecting the physical surroundings is about more than just the room layout. A disorganized room with trash or leftover handouts from a prior presentation does not create a good learning environment. If the room is disordered, participants may transfer this feeling of disorder from the room to the presenter.

Our Training Sessions Are Just Like Vegas!

Creating a healthy learning environment only begins with room selection; the rest of it depends on how we run our training sessions. Specifically, we can promote a more productive learning atmosphere by having an approachable demeanor, fostering participation, and mixing up the pace and style of our teaching.

In other words, a trip to our training sessions should be just like a trip to Vegas: fun, no inhibitions, lots to do, and what happens in training stays in training.

What, you don't see the connection? It's *just like* Vegas!

Having an approachable demeanor is perhaps the most important step toward encouraging learning and openness. When we personalize the material, we make it more memorable and interesting, and we also help the audience identify with us because we let them into our lives. Offering examples and stories from our own experiences—especially challenges we have faced—shows participants that, like them, we also struggle to make exactly the right moves at the right moments. Good practice is also sharing when we have learned something from our audience. This helps model the learning environment behaviors we're encouraging. Acting as though we know everything and we always make the right call tends to isolate the audience, whereas a bit of vulnerability and sharing personal experiences tend to connect us with our audience.

Being approachable as a presenter and encouraging audience participation go hand in hand. If we are approachable, we are more likely to spur audience participation, and audience members tend to feed off one another in that if some audience members are participating, others will likely feel comfortable participating as well. Therefore, starting off strong in this regard is critical. Asking a few questions early in the session and then responding with openly supportive feedback can help audience members feel safe to get involved. These initial audience member comments can also serve as reference points from which we can draw later in the session.

Let's say we've asked a question such as, "What's one of the things you struggle with as a manager?" and Janet pipes up with the following contribution: "Getting employees to go along with a policy they don't see the need for." One way of offering openly supportive feedback might be to say, "Absolutely—don't the rest of you agree? Have you ever experienced this sort of thing?" This response offers the rest of the group an opportunity to identify common ground and to begin to create bonds with one another over shared experiences. If we have a brief example from personal experience, this would be a great opportunity to share it.

The next step is where knowing the names of our audience members can come in handy. With the initial feedback we received to our opening question, we can transition to offering concrete solutions by specifically referencing Janet's contribution: "As Janet has pointed out, gaining buy-in from employees on issues they don't find important can be tough." We succeed in making Janet feel like a vital contributor to the conversation, which in turn will encourage others to participate so that they can gain similar recognition.

Additionally, paraphrasing comments made by participants lets them know we are listening to them and gives them the opportunity to clarify their meaning, thus helping reinforce their contributions. Participants retain more when they're actively involved, so whatever we can do to encourage interaction will be helpful.

As trainers who want to encourage openness and participation, we should also highlight that what happens in training stays in training. This assurance will help people feel that they are in a protected environment where their past mistakes, struggles, or frustrations can be worked out without fear of being talked about around the water cooler the next day.

When soliciting participation, we need to remember that some people will feel more comfortable getting involved than others, so we should avoid putting people on the spot. However, if we are facing a particularly uninvolved group, we have various options for getting people involved:

- Use open-ended questions, which may encourage participation (versus asking yes/no questions). After asking a question, we need to wait and accept the silence; after several seconds of silence, we can then paraphrase the question to see if anyone volunteers an answer.
- Have people pair up to talk about a question, series of questions, or a topic, and then have the pairs report on their conversation.
- Hand out index cards on which people write their responses to discussion questions, and then either collect them and talk about people's responses or have people read aloud what they wrote.
- To encourage more physical participation, we can have everyone stand up, and then ask them to sit down if they agree with a statement. We can then generate conversation based on people's physical responses.
- Similarly, we can designate different corners of the room as possible responses to a given question, and people can go to the corner that best reflects their response to a question. They can then talk among themselves about their response, as well as report out as a group on why they chose that particular corner.
- With a large audience, using small-group activities increases opportunities for participation, especially from people who might otherwise stay quiet in a large group setting.
- When appropriate, we can respond to a partici-

pant's question by polling the entire group to ask for feedback to the question.

- Given that most people have a cell phone these days, we can use sites such as Socrative.com to create questionnaires, or simply poll the audience and receive instant results that everyone can see.

In addition to encouraging participation, we want to encourage questions from the audience. Some folks naturally feel more at ease to jump in and ask a question, but we may want to let our audience know what our preferences are for asking questions. Sometimes, we may want a group to hold onto their questions until we've finished explaining a process in full detail; other times, we'll be okay with people popping their hands up in the middle of the presentation. Communicating our preferences will enable the audience to know whether they should jot down questions as we go along or if they may chime in whenever they have questions.

When audience members ask questions, paraphrasing the question is useful to ensure both that we understand and that the rest of the audience heard the question. Even if the question seems elementary or is about material we just covered, treating questioners politely will encourage the rest of the audience to ask whatever questions they have in mind. If the question asked is off topic, we can volunteer to discuss it with the person at break or at the end of the session.

Train with Pizzazz!

Let's face it: Training can be boring. We've all attended seminars and training sessions that were less than thrilling. Our training sessions need to be different. From the opening through to the closing, we need our training sessions to be engaging and dynamic.

We need to open our presentation with something that will grab our audience's attention and make them want to sit up and listen. Research has shown that audience members decide whether they are going to listen within the first 60-90 seconds of a presentation, meaning that if we don't capture their attention in the beginning, we won't have much chance to do so later.

Here's an idea for an opener that requires active participation from the audience: Hang posters around the room with the major topics of the training session as headings. Distribute sticky notes to the audience members, and ask them to write down questions they have about the topic. They can have multiple questions, but they should include only one question per note. Participants may then post their questions on the appropriate poster by topic heading. This process engages them from the start, enables us to view some of their expectations, and helps the audience feel that something productive will happen.

At end of the training session, learners may retrieve their sticky note if their questions were answered during the session. Ideally, all the notes will be removed, but even if a few are not, we could build in extra time to address such potentials. This format offers a great tool for collaborative reinforcement of learning.

Regardless of the kind of technique we use to open our attention-grabbing attempt—a personal experience, a thought-provoking question, some kind of prop—one of the most crucial aspects of securing audience engagement is enabling them to see what they stand to gain from listening to our material. When we offer tangible ways our information will enhance the lives of audience members, we motivate their curiosity and cause them to mentally stick around to see if we will deliver. Then, of course, we must deliver!

To accomplish a dynamic transfer of training, we must deliver a performance that is both educational and entertaining. Given that people have different learning styles, we need to mix things up by employing a variety of approaches to keep them engaged, including evoking a wide range of emotions throughout a presentation. Audience members especially enjoy some humor and laughter, but we can tap into other emotions as well. Additionally, if we balance explanations of information with demonstrations and applications, the material will more likely appeal to our audience. Because actively engaged participants retain information the best, using inquiry and

DID YOU KNOW?

In Harriet Hankin's book, *The New Workforce: Five Sweeping Trends that Will Shape Your Company's Future,* she writes that "effective communication requires repetition. For the most important messages, once and done will not do."[2]

discovery to lead learners to find answers is often effective.

Enthusiastic body language can also keep the audience more engaged. If we are lethargic, slumping, or shuffling, we are not conveying enthusiasm. John Maxwell's advice is to "act your way into feeling good."[3] This feeling becomes contagious as we look out into an energetic audience. We'll also find that maintaining eye contact is easier with folks who are enjoying our presentation.

We usually find ourselves standing when delivering training, so we want to be sure to convey confidence and enthusiasm through our posture as well. If we plant our feet firmly—without leaning on one leg or the podium—we look more confident and energetic. Standing behind the podium is okay for a portion of the time, but if we stay behind it the entire time, we may seem less confident or interested. Moreover, moving into the audience creates a sense of intimacy with the learners, allowing us to more easily gain and keep their attention.

In addition to using variety with our verbal and nonverbal communication style, we should also break large amounts of information into smaller units. Typically, 15-20 minute segments that alternate between discussions, lectures, and activities work well to maintain attention, and for every 75-90 minutes that we're asking for our audiences' participation and focus, we should intersperse 10-15 minute breaks. This kind of variety requires both including breaks in our agenda as well as carefully watching our audience to see when their attention or energy starts to wane. We can also simply check in with them to determine if they feel the planned breaks seem sufficient.

DID YOU KNOW?

Instead of thinking of those attending as your audience, think of them as "participants." This implies two-way communication instead of one-way.

Regardless of our attention to building in variety and breaks, people inevitably have lapses in their attention, which is why organization and clear transitions are critical during training sessions. Organization and transitions are signals that enable listeners to follow along well. Summaries of key points throughout the session are also useful techniques for recapturing people's attention if they zone out for a few moments. Our goal should be to deliver a concise, memorable message.

Because training sessions sometimes include technical material or jargon, we can easily fall into overusing acronyms and terms that may be unfamiliar to some audience members. Though some acronyms will be natural to our audiences, if we want to make our material memorable, we need to align our choice of language level with that of the audience.

Finally, we should begin and end on time. The material may be scintillating for us to talk about, but staying on track and keeping things moving is essential. Our message should say all that needs to be said and leave out all that does not need to be said—the definition of a concise presenter. This ensures that we clearly align with the training objectives and the agenda set at the beginning of the meeting.

Our closing should be well-thought-out to provide a strong, positive connection of all the issues discussed throughout the session, along with a reminder of why the information will be useful and relevant for the participants. We might also consider issuing a call to action to leave them with some concrete steps to start implementing after the training session.

Providing participants with some kind of takeaway that they can keep with them will increase the likelihood of successful transfer of training. If we provide them with concrete reminders of strategies or steps to perform in different scenarios, they will be much more likely to put into practice the skills covered during training.

It's good practice to keep in touch with the manager of the individuals we trained to informally gauge what impact our training has had and to be able to offer any necessary follow-up. Sometimes transfer of training fails to occur because the participants in the training didn't realize exactly how relevant the material was to their lives, but then once they got back to work they found themselves thinking, "Oh, here's one of those situations that trainer was talking about. Now, what did she say we should do in this kind of case?" Because our handouts or takeaways cannot cover the entire spectrum of reminders audience members might need, providing follow-up support is critical in achieving successful transfer of training.

Chapter 5

Information Updates

Human resources is referred to as the epicenter of the organization. We borrow that word, "epicenter," from earthquake discussions, where the epicenter is the point at which the earthquake begins, and all the following tremors radiate outward from that point. In using this word, then, we mean that human resources acts as a center from which information radiates outward throughout the rest of the organization. As such, the responsibility for driving communication strategy lies with HR professionals.

IN ACTION

Three competencies included in SHRM's Competency Model are relationship management, ethical practice, and critical evaluation.[1] Transparency in information updates is critical in relationship management. Healthy relationships with our stakeholders—both internal and external—depend on honest and ethical communication. Trust can only be fostered by integrity in all we do. HR professionals on the executive level are expected to align organizational strategy with employee advocacy.

Organizational changes are particularly emotional for our workforces and require attention to detail to effectively communicate. Two primary initiatives that prompt the need for specialized communication strategies are downsizings (with layoffs) and mergers and acquisitions. The success of each of these lies with appropriately addressing the "people" issues, which can only be accomplished with a well-planned and well-executed communication strategy. Ironically enough, financial resources are often dedicated to external communication to inform our external stakeholders, but resources are not always dedicated to internal communication—to ensure our employees are kept informed!

The Fastest Way to Explode a Downsizing Effort? Let That Rumor Mill Run

Although organizations engage in downsizing to cut costs, ironically the strategy may actually cost more as a result of increased turnover—if the downsizing is not effectively executed. Organizational survivors will look for opportunities elsewhere if they are dissatisfied. A strong, effective communication strategy can go a long way to retaining more of those individuals.

The advice is to communicate early and often! When layoffs are looming, organizational members often get wind of them informally through the grapevine. If we choose to leave people in the dark rather than forthrightly present them with the facts, the rumor mill will work overtime—and often paint a bleaker picture than the reality of the situation.

Companies often develop strategies to rebuild relationships with external stakeholders, but sometimes the internal "stakeholders"—the employees—are not given the same careful treatment. Because the organizational survivors of layoffs are the ones who will determine if the company will succeed going forward, we must address their needs and concerns directly. When layoffs and restructuring occur, the company changes: It essentially becomes a different company than it was before. Therefore, we need to acknowledge the changes and openly discuss them.

Human resources must champion this cause on behalf of the employees for whom they serve

DID YOU KNOW?

"Laid-off workers who understand how layoff decisions were made and believe that they were treated fairly are more likely to recommend their former employer to others. They also are more willing to return to work for them, Temple University researchers have found."[2]

—*Dori Meinert*

as advocates. No one wants to be the bearer of bad news, yet if we remain silent, distrust skyrockets. Therefore, we need to communicate, communicate, and communicate some more! The attitude of "business as usual" after a downsizing is toxic.

As HR professionals, we also need to ensure that senior management is visible throughout the process. Employees need to talk about the changes—preferably with management—and to create new working relationships. These organizational survivors cannot be simply told to "get over it" because many times they are doing more work with fewer resources, they have lost co-workers and friends, and they are dealing with a wide range of emotions. Management, therefore, needs to communicate two main things: empathy and the path forward.

The best way to communicate the path forward is through regular face-to-face meetings in which we explain—with as much candor as we can afford—how decisions were made. Honest communication means not only sharing what we know but also admitting what we don't know. If we openly share the rationale for the downsizing, we can help employees better understand the situation. They might not like or agree with the rationale, but at least if they know it, they will be able to evaluate it for themselves instead of being forced to make up reasons as to why the layoffs occurred and what else might happen next.

Newsletters and the company intranet may be useful supplements to the face-to-face meetings, but they should not replace in-person communication because it is the avenue through which employees will most perceive our sensitivity to their plight.

During difficult times such as these, we need to deliver difficult messages and be comfortable doing so. We'll be operating in a fish bowl where everything we say and do is under scrutiny, so there are a few important ways we can strengthen our communication. First, we must not make false promises. During layoffs, employees experience a loss of trust, so they will be reassessing their colleagues to determine whom they consider trustworthy. Our job is to prove to them that we are a reliable advocate for them, working hard to keep them current as all the details unfold.

Because downsizing is stressful for us as well, we must keep a positive attitude and communicate it to employees. We do not have to sing "The sun'll come out tomorrow" or be unrealistic about the situation, but we must work against the tendency for people to become disillusioned and pessimistic about the company. This kind of work environment will cause many of the organizational survivors to want to leave, which will make a bad situation that much worse.

Instead, we need to work to create a team atmosphere bent on surviving and thriving. "We" should be the pronoun of choice so that unity is emphasized; avoiding the proverbial "they" will help in not vilifying senior management. As well, using employees' first names during organizational upheaval reinforces the fact that we really view ourselves as in the trenches with them. An often-overlooked priority during such events is recognizing employees when they are doing a good job. Acknowledging their efforts sends messages of affirmation and hope during the turmoil, confirming that they are still valuable to the company.

Additionally, we need to have a vision of how the newly downsized company will look so that we can clearly articulate it to the employees who remain. Before any presentation to employees, we must know our facts, prepare our remarks, and practice saying exactly what needs to be said. We also need to communicate well with line managers, as they are often on the front lines of fielding the day-to-day questions. Employees will inevitably ask these managers lots of questions, so they need to be properly informed.

All communication is a two-way street, so we shouldn't assume that we'll do all the talking. Employees should feel free to ask questions and offer feedback. We don't experience the company from the same angle as they do, so getting their feedback can be invaluable. Some feedback will come from negative feelings about the layoffs and downsizing, so it's important that we have a thick skin and don't take employee feedback personally. Even if their perspective is tainted by their negative emotions, they will likely offer some grains of truth. As well, we should take responsibility and resist the temptation to shift the blame.

DID YOU KNOW?

According to Joelle Jay in the article, "Focus on 5 Key Strategies to Improve Communication Skills," we must "know when to stop talking and start listening." Furthermore, "people feel acknowledged when others validate their feelings, and when managers ignore feelings, they create distance between themselves and their employees."[3]

If we are open, honest, responsible, and decisive, we can show employees that we are trustworthy advocates during this time of change.

Finally, we must address the emotions people are inevitably feeling: Uncertainty, stress, and anxiety are the prevailing emotions of organizational survivors. How we treat our employees—laid off as well as remaining—will be a critical factor determining whether our downsizing will be successful. The knee-jerk reaction is often to shut down employee interaction and try to prohibit negative talk. But the fact is, they need to talk. Acknowledging the stressful and emotional nature of this situation is important, and doing so will confirm our empathy toward the employees and their situation. Part of acknowledging the emotions they feel includes acknowledging the fact that we alone are not equipped to help everyone who might need help. Therefore, we should remind them of any employee assistance programs or counseling services that might be available to them.

Many times, people who survive traumatic events together create stronger bonds with one another. Once the downsizing and layoffs are over, we need to communicate this information across the organization so that everyone can breathe a sigh of relief. Although things won't return to normal overnight, and the road to recovering stability, trust, and morale will be long, if we commit to consistent, honest, face-to-face communication and empathy, we can hope that we will emerge from the layoffs stronger and healthier than before.

Where Not to Communicate with Employees: The Local Paper

As with layoffs and downsizing, communication is the cornerstone of a well-executed merger or acquisition strategy, and it needs to begin early with the due diligence phase. The communication strategy is actually part of the deal.

Most mergers and acquisitions fail as a result of human issues. Intuitively, it should make sense that our human capital (a critical constituency) should be addressed in a merger or acquisition. And yet, any communication budget is generally spent externally, instead of on our employees.

In the beginning, the communication is all about awareness. Then the focus shifts to providing a road map for the future direction. The next phase emphasizes how the change is affecting the workforce, and the final phase provides the details of how it will be executed. Keeping these phases in mind will help us frame our messages to the workforce.

One of the first crucial moves is timing and coordinating the announcements. We should not release information externally before it is shared internally. We also need to ensure that the acquired, acquiring, or merging companies all distribute consistent messages. The internal communication must be shared *before* the external communication begins, and it needs to be shared with the same detail as employees will read in their local newspapers. We do not want our workforce getting its information about what is going on from the local paper! It's a myth to think that we are protecting employees and keeping morale and productivity up by hiding the truth from them. The reality is just the opposite: Blindsiding employees will cost us dearly in both morale and productivity—not to mention trust! If we hide one thing, employees will naturally wonder what else we are hiding. Transparency is a much better policy than secrecy.

Peggy Eddens, Executive Vice President & Chief Human Capital Officer at WSFS Bank in Delaware, tells a story about flying out of Pittsburgh for a former employer during a snowstorm so she could tell employees in person about a potential sale of the company.[4] She arrived at her destination in the midst of an ice storm and had to literally crawl across the ice-covered parking lot to her rental car, but she was determined to deliver the announcement before it hit the newsstands the next morning. This step was just the first of many in communicating the importance of the workforce during this transition. The payoff? Little to no turnover during the transition and a valuation significantly higher than expected! That's a worthwhile investment.

With change, face-to-face communication is imperative because many employees will want to see us talk through the details so they can evaluate how truthful they think we are. In-person meetings should be a continuous process, with employee questions and concerns driving some of the announcements and information. As with layoffs, we'll need to hold regular briefings for managers as well, and we may want to create a supplemental newsletter devoted to the topic, in which interviews with top executives could be shared. Our workforce may not agree with the strategic decisions, but we must respect them enough to provide them with open, honest communication about the decision so they can understand it.

Be careful not to minimize the situation with potentially disingenuous comments such as, "It's not that bad" or "It'll all be over soon." We need to be truthful and share with employees exactly how they will be affected by the merger or acquisition. Employees will no doubt be wondering about some of the same things: Is there job security? Is my job changing? Is my job moving? Will I have a new manager? What is the impact on my compensation? The key is to minimize uncertainty by anticipating questions and by offering employees as much as we know and are able to tell them.

We can also create additional mechanisms for addressing questions and concerns. Focus groups may be a useful means of soliciting more feedback and keeping the channels of communication open. Smaller groups provide more opportunities for sharing, and they also give us the opportunity to take action if a question reveals an issue we had not thought of.

As well, we should encourage and allow employees to take some responsibility. We need to avoid the victim role ourselves and urge employees not to fall into this mode of thinking either. Having employees take some responsibility will also give them a feeling of control.

We may feel our own set of emotions, but we need to resist showing frustration with employees or being confrontational. We need to control our language, which may mean pausing longer than normal before speaking. This will help us consider the best way to phrase our responses so that we avoid sarcasm, belittling, or instigating. The long pause will help us turn "Yeah, well so's your face!" into a more tactful reply such as, "That's an interesting point. I understand why you might come to that conclusion."

When the Competition Becomes the Colleague

Post-merger communication is also critical. This phase requires gaining buy-in for the vision of the "new" organization. Even after the deal, the companies are still integrating the two organizations and the two cultures.

All the recommendations about layoffs and downsizing apply to mergers and acquisitions, but a key difference between the two is the fact that the new organization will not be a smaller version of the original, but a blended version in which two cultures have been forced to forego their old culture and begin to create a new one—often with people who replaced friends and colleagues. This situation creates a particular challenge for the HR professional.

Team building rises to the top of our priorities list because we'll need to begin to build new relationships and establish new norms. Many of the strategies listed in Chapter 3 on welcoming new employees will provide useful ways of connecting employees to one another.

However, we should not ignore the fact that the work environment is sometimes inherently awkward and therefore strained after a merger or acquisition has been completed. Part of the assimilation process will include acknowledging this fact and moving forward in light of it. One concrete way of doing this is to celebrate milestones along the way. When the new company meets its first goal or survives its first quarter, we should celebrate its achievements to create new memories and traditions and to continue taking us down the path toward establishing a new normal.

Whether our company is facing downsizing or a merger, these kinds of situations will test our professional communication skills in a way unlike many other scenarios we face on the job. Honesty, frequency, and empathy in talking with employees will be critical factors contributing to our success.

Chapter 6

The Interview

Identify your company's biggest competitor. Imagine that late one night, you hear a knock on the door, and standing on your doorstep is the brains behind its operation.

"Wanna know the secret to our success?" she asks you, kind of bragging.

"Why would you want to reveal that?" you ask, feeling a little suspicious—oh, and tired too, since she just dragged you out of bed.

"Oh, just so you understand why your company will always struggle and our company will always thrive."

Well, that's obnoxious, so of course you want to know the company's secret so you can use it to your advantage and put her out of business. You answer, "Okay, sure," while imagining buying her Mercedes at an estate sale once she goes bankrupt.

Corralling you into said Mercedes, she speeds silently through the night to her office building. Then she leads you down a small flight of stairs at the back of the building to a seemingly secret room. Now your breath is coming quicker; you're starting to get excited.

You wonder what could possibly be waiting behind that door—some high-tech microchip? A special serum that makes their people wicked-smart? The Rancor Monster from "Return of the Jedi" that eats anyone who comes close to challenging the company's success? What could it be? And is she really going to just give up the information that has sealed the company's competitive edge?

You do not have to wait long because she shoves the door open and pushes you inside for a look.

Bright light spills out into the hallway, and you stand there frozen in the doorway, blinking to adjust your eyes, shocked. The room is full of people who hardly notice you have entered. Just inside are rows of cubicles with people busily typing on their keyboards or talking into their headsets. Farther into the room, at a large table in the middle, about a half dozen people are busily examining a graphic you cannot quite make out. You're stunned. This is it? Their secret weapon is a bunch of hard workers?

Now you realize why she brought you here: It's because even if you know the secret to their success, it's not as if you can just steal a microchip and the secret weapon is yours.

The War for Talent

Acquiring and retaining dynamic employees is an art.

These days, more and more businesses are realizing that the real war is not so much about who has the most information or the best gadgets, but who has the most talented people. In reality, the company that is winning the talent war will end up collecting the best information or producing the coolest gadgets anyway.

Every organization is waging an ongoing battle in the war for talent. Though organizations have access to roughly the same technology and the same information, it's crucial to remember that *people* make the difference. People are the source of our competitive advantage! And if this is the case, then the interview process is one of the most crucial investments a company can make.

IN ACTION

The interview provides an opportunity for the HR professional to "demonstrate an understanding of the strategic relationship between effective human resource management and core business functions,"[1] as identified by SHRM's business acumen competency. Furthermore, the HR professional "serves as an in-house workforce and people management expert"[2] when filling the consultation competency.

To win the war for talent requires that we be skilled in selecting, recruiting, and engaging that talent. We have less room for error than ever before. Only with effective communication skills are we able to maximize our "hits" and minimize our "misses." A hit is not just hiring that great applicant, but it is also not hiring the problematic one. On the flip side, our misses are hiring the person we should have passed on or not hiring the A-performer who went on to put his or her outstanding skill set to work for our competitor. Mistakes in the hiring arena come with large price tags for the organization, whether in terms of missed opportunities or actual financial costs trying to terminate a poor performer. Some estimates suggest the cost of a bad hire is far more than the yearly salary of the position.

The selection process today goes beyond the person-job fit. Now it's a three-pronged approach consisting of the person-job-organization fit. To determine the applicant's fit with the organization's culture often requires communication on a deeper level than simply reading qualifications on a resume or application. Our communication needs to engage the applicant in conversation that draws out the individual's personality so that we can see his or her strengths and weaknesses.

Furthermore, we know that the interview process is a two-way street. As we interview applicants, they are "interviewing" us and sizing up our organization to see if it fits. It's not just the applicants who need to offer a stellar performance: We do too! And delivering a great performance means communicating strategically throughout the preparation, interview, and follow-up phases of the interview process.

Preparation Is Half the Battle

The preparation phase is mostly about strong nonverbal communication. When we are well prepared for an interview, the applicant will get the message that we are courteous professionals, we have an engaging job to fill, and we work for a dynamic company.

Preparation sends a positive message. If we have read the applicant's resume and have it at our fingertips (not buried in a pile we have to shuffle through), we communicate a degree of professionalism that most applicants appreciate. We can also better identify those areas of interest to probe when we have prepared by reading the resume. Finally, being prepared tells applicants that we value them and their time.

Some of the nonverbal elements that affect the interview include the physical surroundings. Just as we are searching the candidate for clues to confirm he or she is the right one for the job, the candidate is also searching for clues to confirm that this is the right environment for him or her. A disorganized workspace or a lack of seating for the applicant (until a space is cleared) may communicate that the interviewer is ill-prepared and may throw doubt on the orderliness of the company itself. The interviewee may begin to wonder if this is a snapshot of the way the entire company runs. These are messages we must avoid when waging the war for talent.

In today's open office plans, many interviewers don't have private offices, so conference rooms are a wise choice to ensure privacy. In most cases, they need to be reserved in advance, so we need to add this task to our preparation list. Strategically, booking the room for a little longer than the anticipated interview time is best because no one—interviewer or interviewee—wants the meeting interrupted by a knock at the door from the next group that has reserved the room. A misfortune of this kind would probably not impress our prospective new hire. The last benefit of using a conference room is the features it usually has and does not have: a door, but no office phone or computer. This combination wards off distractions and provides the best chance for an uninterrupted conversation.

Last, every effort should be made to start and end the interview on time. If we're late for the appointment, we may send the message that we feel the interview is of secondary importance. In the case of an emergency, we may contact the applicant, apologize, explain the issue as much as we are able to, and then offer to meet later or schedule another time. We never want to leave applicants sitting and waiting; in the war for talent, they may just be a critical component to our organization's future success.

Introduction to the Interview

An interview is a moment for us to draw out the best in the person whom we've chosen to spend time interviewing. By time an applicant is coming for an interview, we have dedicated a lot of resources to getting that person in front of us, so we want to enable that person to show off his or

DID YOU KNOW?

Nonverbal communications expert Albert Mehrabian produced a study reporting that when listening to a speaker, 55 percent of the message comes from body language, 38 percent of it comes from the intonation, and only 7 percent of the message we take away comes from the speaker's words.[3]

her strengths. We can take some practical steps with our body language and our words to draw out an applicant's personality; these steps will allow us to listen and observe who this person is and where his or her strengths and weaknesses lie.

Nonverbally, one of the best things we can do to set people at ease is to greet them warmly as if we're glad to see them. Greeting candidates warmly means standing up and walking toward them with a smile. Staying seated in our chair and simply waving the person in communicates that we're in the middle of something else instead of looking forward to the interview. Another essential aspect to a warm greeting is addressing people by name and pronouncing it correctly, along with identifying ourselves to avoid any confusion. Finally, the greeting should involve a firm handshake.

Many a job has been lost on the basis of a handshake; however, this cuts both ways and applies to the interviewer as well as the interviewee, women as well as men. A weak finger-tip brush is not a handshake. A limp, squishy hand offering is not a handshake. A handshake should be firm and palm to palm—two pumps are sufficient. But the firmness should not be overdone as in an arm-wrestling match. Think about how firmly you grasp the lid of a jar that has already been opened. It's not with the same vigor that you wrench open a sealed jar. Our interviewee's hand is not an unopened jar lid, and if we hear knuckles popping or leave ring indentations, we've overdone it. We should offer a firm handshake at the beginning and ending of interviews to serve as a physical demonstration that we are glad to meet the candidates and are looking forward to engaging conversation.

As a final component in the nonverbal aspects of the introduction to the interview, we should also give thought to possible physical barriers to the communication process. When conducting the interview in our office, it is easiest—and more comfortable for us—to sit back behind the desk; however, this nonverbal message is similar to having our arms crossed across our chest: The message is that we're distant and a little cold. If we are using a conference room, we might be tempted to sit across the table from the applicant. To be more open, we should instead consider an informal seating arrangement where we can sit corner to corner, which would indicate a more collaborative relationship. This is our goal if we view the interview process as a means by which we can partner with new talent.

Verbally, one of the first things we can do to make applicants feel comfortable and welcome is to begin with some small talk about who they are. Though this interaction may not feel germane to the interview, we can actually learn a great deal about applicants from their personal background and how they talk about that background.

Additionally, opening up and talking a bit about our own background can help set interviewees at ease. Some folks feel more comfortable talking about what they know—themselves; others feel more comfortable hearing about the person with whom they are speaking. Another benefit to talking about ourselves is that it makes us feel more approachable and relatable to interviewees so that they don't feel as if we are an impersonal automaton simply making decisions based on resume bullet points.

The Heart of the Interview

As a signal that the interview is officially beginning (after the preliminary conversational questions), interviewers may want to outline the agenda for applicants so they know what to expect. Providing an agenda helps interviewees feel like there won't be any surprises, and it shows our competence and our awareness of the time frame in which we're operating.

We can also set candidates at ease by not furiously writing throughout the interview. If we must take notes, jotting a quick word or symbol here or there is usually sufficient without being obtrusive, and it will help make interviews feel more like personal conversations. This technique may take some careful planning and strategy ahead of time on our part. For instance, if we jot down attributes we're looking for or questions we have, we can then check items off our list or write "yes" or "no" next to the questions. Plusses or minuses also work great in this kind of scenario.

Just as our main goal with our verbal and nonverbal language is to reduce anxiety and to show interest and engagement, we can use our language in nonthreatening ways when we ask questions. In the role of the interviewer, we will ask lots of questions, but how we ask those questions—the language and phrasing we use—can distinguish a friendly, comfortable interview from one that feels threatening and dangerous or competitive. This is not an interrogation, so using a softer style is usually beneficial in making applicants feel safe to open up.

Asking questions that reflect information from applicants' resumes lets them know that we've done our homework; in addition, the best predictor of future performance is past performance. An effective tool for encouraging people to talk is to ask about past experiences; talking about familiar events helps set individuals at ease. These provide insight into how candidates approached situations in the past and thus how they might approach them in the future.

Although we may think we know answers to some of the questions, we must take care to phrase them objectively and avoid leading questions. Open-ended questions provide the applicant with an opportunity to talk more—and for us to listen more. For example, an unassuming question for a candidate who already has managerial experience might be, "Have you ever had to terminate an employee?" instead of "Can you tell me about a time when you had to terminate an employee?" The difference is slight, but the former question is unassuming, whereas the latter is assuming.

Additionally, "have you ever" questions are less formal and are more likely to occur in everyday life. They have the potential to encourage interviewees to relax some and share more than they might have if we had phrased the questions more formally. The responses to these questions about candidates' past behavior provide valuable insight into their likely future behavior.

Once we've asked about past experiences, we have potentially readied candidates for hypothetical behavioral and situational interview questions. Hypothetical questions allow us to create our own complex scenarios to see how applicants think on their feet.

For example, if interviewing someone for a supervisor position, we might ask, "How would you handle discovering that an employee had been stealing from your cash drawer on a regular basis?" The phrase, "how would you handle," is strategically vague and implies that we want to hear about the range of actions the applicant would take, instead of just a single action. Asking the question, "What would you do if you discovered an employee stealing from the cash drawer on a regular basis?" runs the risk of eliciting a single action answer: "I'd fire the person." We would then have to ask follow-up questions to draw out a more complex answer. Although the applicant might still only say, "Fire the person," to our "How would you handle" question, our hope is that this kind of question will elicit a more detailed answer.

Our goal is to gain insight into applicants' thought processes and help them talk freely, but we must steer clear of illegal or inappropriate information that may create a legal minefield. Most applicants know and adhere to general rules of decorum, but there will always be people who somehow manage to tell us, with a wink, that they "didn't inhale" or otherwise divulge too much information about their personal lives. It's a good idea to devise a standard plan for how we'll bring these conversations back on track. The most subtle way of doing this is simply to break eye contact by looking down at the papers in front of us and shift our shoulders slightly away from the speaker. This strategy communicates that we're thinking about the next question or item on our agenda.

Of course, someone who would bring up inappropriate information in the middle of an interview might not be well versed in the subtleties of nonverbal communication. In this case, the direct approach will be necessary, and a simple clearing of the throat might serve to give the applicant pause in the middle of a story, at which point we might say something such as, "Another thing I found interesting about your resume is . . ."

No matter how strategic we are with our verbal communication, if it does not agree with our nonverbal communication, our words will be disregarded in favor of the message being sent by our actions. Thus, making sure that our facial expressions and body language are open and supportive is crucial.

Our facial expressions throughout the interview should remain positive and engaged—attentive and generally interested in what the person is saying and feeling. To be specific, our eyebrows communicate quite a bit about our level of engagement: When we are thinking along with them and attempting to show concentration, our eyebrows furrow and go down; however, when we are engaged and interested, our eyebrows are up, widening our eyes and making us look more enthusiastic. It is also a truism that smiling will make interviewees feel more at ease and encouraged to open up.

Maintaining open body language often puts applicants at ease as well, and perhaps makes them more likely to mirror that openness. Because we want them to feel our interest in them and their story, our body language must communicate openness and encourage disclosure. We can do this in a number of different ways. First, squaring our shoulders to applicants shows that we are locked into the conversation and are listening attentively to what the applicants say.

Moreover, sitting up straight—perhaps even leaning toward the person slightly—and not slumping or slouching communicates our interest and engagement with the conversation. We can also unbutton our jacket if applicable and avoid crossing our arms. Crossed arms—and sometimes crossed legs—make us seem closed off to interviewees and may cause them to feel that we are unapproachable and distant. Taking care not to fiddle with paperclips or pens or anything in front of us is another measure to prevent us from seeming preoccupied during interviews.

Often the little things can make a difference in continuing to put our interviewees at ease. Offering food or something to drink, if appropriate, may help. As well, politeness may dictate that we open the door for interviewees if we're show them around the office; however, when we open the door and insist that interviewees go through first, they may feel uncomfortable being in the lead and not knowing where they're going. Instead, we may simply want to walk through the door first and hold it open for interviewees to proceed through the door behind us.

Any person we encounter in the office with our interviewee needs to be properly and warmly introduced. However, we should avoid conducting personal or long-winded conversations with co-workers while interviewees are present to avoid causing our guests unnecessary discomfort or making them think we are uninterested in continuing the interview.

Taking care to communicate our interest and engagement with our candidates can put them at ease

DID YOU KNOW?

"Like all difference, generalizations about generational differences should be used only as guidelines to help you understand what might be preventing understanding. Your goal should be to move from the categories…to the people themselves… quickly and accurately."[4]

—*Kate Berardo and Simma Lieberman*

and enable them to show us what they are made of—both good and bad—so that we can be better positioned to spot talent and avoid poor hiring choices.

The Close and After

Once we've asked all our questions, two things generally happen: We transition into talking about the position and the company, and then we ask if the applicant has any questions. These moments are just as important in the interview process because they are the points at which we need to sell the company to the interviewee.

If any portion of the interview is likely to sound canned, it's the discussion of the position and company because we will have described the company many, many times by now. Because we don't want to sound as though we're reading from the annual report or the company website, we will need to make the discussion more personal and offer applicants insight into what working at the company is really like. It'll be helpful to think ahead of time about the kinds of stories we might tell that will provide a realistic yet favorable and personal view of the company and our experiences there.

When the tables are turned and we are asked questions, we need to answer the questions honestly to again give candidates a reasonable snapshot of life at the company. If a question feels over the line or puts us in an awkward position, the key is to remain diplomatic and still end on a positive note. Ending on a high provides an incentive for candidates to return, if invited.

The final element of the close should be a clear outline of the rest of the process so that the applicant knows what to expect and what kind of time line is reasonable. Our responsibility is to stick to that time line or let candidates know about any delays. This portion of the process speaks just as loudly about us and our company.

Alternate Interview Formats

The face-to-face interview remains the most popular selection tool for making hiring decisions, and it often receives a disproportionate emphasis in the process. Plenty of other tools—from personality tests to aptitude and ability tests—are available by which to identify new talent. Ironically, research has concluded that the interview is among the least reliable selection tools. For one thing, research indicates that the decision whether to hire an applicant is made within the first 60-90 seconds of the interview. Unfortunately, very little of the applicant's qualifications are discussed in this first minute or two, so we must be careful to maintain objectivity and avoid biased judgments.

Maintaining objectivity and avoiding bias begins with self-awareness. Though certain classes (such as women, minorities, or people with disabilities) are protected by federal, state, and local legislation, our biases may go far beyond that. Today's biases include "beautyism," dress, smokers, weight, and sexual orientation. Care should be taken to avoid negative stereotypes and disparaging language.

Some companies have found other strategies for identifying and recruiting talent, including team interviews and group interviews.

With a higher level of inter-rater reliability, team interviews have increased dramatically in use. A team interview is when a panel of employees interviews a single applicant. As you might imagine, this format requires coordination to make it work. Planning and preparation are required to ensure that the interviewers are not talking over one another and that each is assigned a primary area of responsibility to make certain all topics are covered.

These team or panel interviews are sometimes referred to as stress interviews, and for good reason. For an already anxious applicant, we multiply the anxiety by adding to the number of people who must be impressed. Logistically, a single person should be identified to greet applicants and bring them to the room where the other panelists are waiting. This individual can engage in some small talk to put candidates at ease and then introduce the panel members. To communicate support and serve as the point person for the interview, this person should sit next to the applicants (since sitting alongside is more collaborative).

Applicants should be told before entering the room that a panel awaits. The more advance notice for candidates, the better.

Using the stress interview (or at least asking some high-stress questions) is particularly useful in determining how candidates handle pressure. And realistically, this is an important prerequisite for most positions today!

In a group interview, a company invites multiple applicants to be interviewed in a group setting. Disney and ToysRUs are two of the larger companies that have successfully used this technique, and although it requires additional interviewers in the room to observe the interaction between the candidates, this kind of strategy may be useful in evaluating job applicants for how well they'll fit in with the culture of the company.

As we leverage technology more and more to cut the costs of recruiting, the Skype interview has gained in popularity. Skype also provides the option of recording the interview, which may be helpful in obtaining multiple perspectives on an applicant's fit for the position. However, this is a form of face-to-face interviewing that, to be successful, requires some patience and finesse to ensure that the technology does not get in the way of providing a platform for interviewees.

For starters, usernames should be shared a few days in advance so that each party feels prepared for the contact. We should also use a company account (versus our personal account, "boldbrassybeautiful") to maintain a level of professionalism and anonymity—interviewees shouldn't be able to use Skype to call us back at home in a week to check in on why they have not received a callback.

We should also do a few practice runs with the technology so that we feel comfortable using it. Just as in a face-to-face interview, our ability to pull it off smoothly will speak well or ill of our company.

The location selection is critical. We might consider a quiet office or a conference room that has a blank wall with the company logo visible. Whatever location we choose, the camera should not show our mile-high pile of messy papers teetering on the desk behind us. Distractions should be avoided, just as if the candidate were sitting in front of us, so we will need to consider our outfit, the lighting, and the placement of the camera. Computers can strangely pixilate colors and patterns, so on camera our checked blouse or bright blue tie might cause sensory overload on the other end of the Skype conversation.

Interviews of all kinds offer HR professionals the opportunity to tangibly increase company value, one person at a time. The key to winning the war for talent is recruiting and retaining the right people, and if we carefully prepare and communicate well, we will score the hits and minimize the misses.

Chapter 7

Delivering Feedback

Close your eyes for a moment, and imagine with us a workplace where the new hire came on board and performed her job exactly as she was asked, where the veteran employee never forgot to add that one column of numbers in his report, where even the copy machine repair folks showed up right when you needed them. Now open your eyes. Darn—that ruined it, didn't it?

Unfortunately, the bad news is that people will always do certain parts of their jobs worse than expected; however, the good news is that some people will do certain parts of their jobs better than expected. This is why we need performance appraisals: They enable organizations to see where people are excelling and where they need a little nudge. Without performance appraisals, companies would have a hard time identifying and nurturing new talent. As well, they might find providing constructive feedback to struggling employees even more difficult.

These two prongs are what make performance appraisals so important: the developmental prong and the administrative one. As a developmental tool, the performance appraisal provides vital feedback to the employee, recognizing strengths, weaknesses, and training opportunities. As an administrative tool, it serves as documentation for HR decisions such as promotions, terminations, and staffing needs.

Perhaps the fact that so much hinges on the performance evaluation is what makes it one of the most dreaded management tasks. Many managers feel that they have been thrust into positions—with no preparation or guidance—and told to evaluate their employees' performance.

Research has reported that one of the key reasons cited for employees leaving organizations is their disappointment with the performance appraisal process and poor ratings they received. The message is that doing a better job with performance appraisals can be a retention tool for organizations, ultimately saving them money. However, for the appraisal process to be successful, two things are needed: open, two-way communication to minimize the power dynamic and an emphasis on the value and usefulness of the review. These two things need to be our focus as we prepare for, deliver, and follow up on performance reviews.

IN ACTION

Relationship management and consultation are two particularly important competencies involved in effectively delivering feedback.[1] Successfully holding difficult conversations with employees requires that HR professionals provide a line of sight for individuals to the overall business goals. This will help build the business case for the changes the employees need to make. And feedback must be delivered in a mutually respectful manner.

It's All in the Setup

Setting the tone for the performance appraisal interview begins before the appraisal even occurs. We can communicate so much to employees simply by the way we schedule the interviews, how much time we allot, and what location we choose.

The performance appraisal begins with how the interview is scheduled. To convey the importance of the process and send a clear message to employees, the invitation to the interview should be delivered professionally. In other words, a passing comment in the hall will not suffice and will instead send the message that for both the evaluator and the evaluated, this process is just another hoop they both have to jump through. Delivering the invitation professionally means we need either to send an official e-mail invitation or to stop by in person to schedule the event.

One of the things that make managers uncomfortable with the evaluation process is that it draws attention to the power dynamic between the supervisor and the subordinate. This feeling is natural, but there are ways to minimize its effects. For example, in the set-up phase, instead of just telling employees the date the appraisal is scheduled, we can offer a few dates and ask employees which one would work best for them. Doing so enables people to feel as though they have some say in the process, and it's not just going to be a top-down procedure in which they won't have a voice.

During a face-to-face chat or e-mail exchange about scheduling the appraisal, we will also have the opportunity to describe the evaluation process. Communicating up front what the performance appraisal will look and sound like creates at least two positive benefits: It allows employees to ask any questions they might have, and it highlights the significance of the appraisal.

Answering questions in the initial phase of the process is another way of signaling to employees that the appraisal will not be a one-sided conversation. Hopefully it will also encourage concerns to surface and be addressed ahead of time so that the actual meeting may be as tension-free as possible.

Highlighting the importance of the appraisal is crucial from the outset because employees need to see how valuable it is in our eyes and how potentially valuable it can be for them. When we describe the process and answer questions about it, we have the opportunity to communicate what benefits can be gained from all the parties involved. The company stands to benefit from the evaluation, the employee stands to benefit, and—if we are willing—we stand to benefit. Naturally, any description of the appraisal process should connect the dots between the company's goals and values and the specific areas that will be discussed during the appraisal. Letting employees know this information ahead of time will help it sink in and potentially make the appraisal more meaningful.

If employees see how the appraisal aligns with the company goals, they may also see how the appraisal can work to their advantage. A positive appraisal will communicate to the company that they are valuable assets who further the company's mission; a negative appraisal will help them identify the areas they need to work harder on to improve their value to the company. Communicating the usefulness of the appraisal to employees in advance gives them a lens through which to view the process when it occurs and may potentially make the official meeting more productive.

One last powerful way we can emphasize the significance of the performance appraisal is to communicate how useful the process is to us personally. Specifically, we can offer our own appraisal experiences, but even more valuable is to tell our employees that we learn from them during the review process. Of course, this statement must actually be true. But hopefully it won't take too much to convince you that thinking through someone else's work habits, styles, and methods may be very instructive. No matter how long we've been doing our job, watching what someone else does while they are doing their job can always teach us something—even if it's something small.

As HR professionals, we have the great benefit of analyzing lots of different ways of working, so we have the opportunity to continually tweak our own work styles based on the things we learn from others. Genuinely communicating this benefit to the people we evaluate will make us seem more human to them. We won't be a distant administrator sitting across a desk from them, telling them how they fall short; instead, we'll be teammates, sitting alongside each other, learning from each other how we can each become more sharply skilled at our craft. The result will be setting up the performance appraisal to be viewed as it should: a powerful tool for growth.

In addition to carefully thinking through how we talk to employees about the appraisal process, we will also communicate its value by how much time we allocate for it. We all take our cue about the importance of an event by the time set aside. When scheduling a performance evaluation interview, a failure to set aside enough time communicates nonverbally that the process (or the employee) is not important. If we only manage to allot 15 minutes, squeezed in between a meeting on one side and a conference call on the other, employees will feel that rush and assume that the evaluation discussion is an inconvenience at best.

Furthermore, the location of the meeting similarly communicates its relevance. A private setting with no interruptions is essential. We all know how tempting a ding from our phone or computer can be, and some of us are more distracted by office traffic and conversations than others. Continual glances out a doorway or at a computer screen are clear nonverbal cues that tell the people we're with that something else is on our minds.

DID YOU KNOW?

Paul Harris reported in "Harnessing the Zeal of the Millennial Generation" that Millennials "require an abundance of attention in general and specific guidance in particular about their career aspirations."[2]

We therefore need to choose our location strategically and think through the preparations we must make to ensure that we will be fully present when discussing each employee's job performance. And by the way, a special location can simply be our office, but arranged in a different way than normal—with the computer screen off, phones silenced, two chairs comfortably near one another, and no distracting paperwork on our desk. When the people being appraised see the care we have taken in creating an interruption- and distraction-free location, they will see yet another confirmation that this process means a great deal to us, them, and the company.

Delivering the News

Before we talk about the nuts and bolts of how we can effectively conduct performance reviews, it's a good idea to consider our mental state going into a review. We should take a few minutes before each review to mentally prepare in at least two ways: remove our natural biases and do something enjoyable.

We all find certain people more interesting, attractive, and winsome than others, but in a performance evaluation, allowing those biases to go unchecked can land us in court. Therefore, we need to take a few moments before each review to remind ourselves of both the goals of the review and the humanity of the person we'll be speaking with. Remembering that the review is supposed to draw out the best in the people being evaluated will help us avoid unfairly criticizing the people we're not as fond of and buttering up the people we like. Reviewing the goals and values of the company and how our conversation is specifically going to reinforce those goals will help guide our actions during the appraisal. We should also remember that our employees are human and have similar values, desires, and concerns as the rest of us. Remembering that they share many of the same values we do—even if they're expressed completely differently—will help us talk to them with the courtesy and respect they deserve.

To help get us in the right frame of mind and stay there, doing something enjoyable right before the meeting is often useful. Because the conversation will require a positive tone, shaking off the concerns and stresses of the day may help us approach the evaluation with renewed energy. The break doesn't need to take much time as long as it improves our mood—from stretching, to listening to music, to brewing a fresh cup of coffee; whatever it is, discover it, and use it.

And now for the part everyone has been waiting for. If we have set up the appraisal well, maybe—just maybe—both parties will feel a bit of anticipation mixed in with all the other feelings of dread, loathing, and whatever else people bring to such meetings. As important as the setup is to the process, the delivery is what ultimately matters. So we need to give some strategic thought to how we'll welcome each employee, deliver the good news, offer the suggestions, and close the meeting.

We've all gotten that wave-from-behind-the-desk-while-on-the-phone-and-checking-the-computer. It says anything from, "Come on in, but not really" to "Ugh! You again! And on today of all days!" Needless to say, this is not the best way to start the encounter.

Opening up the process has that "first impression" kind of magnitude to it. If employees' first impression is that we are busy, they will not feel comfortable for the duration of the conversation. Because we carved out time and carefully selected a location for this meeting, we should also be able to take time to prepare for our employees' arrival. Having the appropriate paperwork ready and completed and the seating arrangement set up will provide a positive signal to the incoming person that we're ready for and anticipating this process.

Our initial welcoming should be the same as that of a job interview: Stand up, smile warmly, shake hands while welcoming the person, and then offer the person a seat. We've mentioned the seating considerations in other chapters, but the key is that we should take some time to consider whether our seating arrangement reinforces or dismantles the power dynamic we referred to earlier in this chapter. Consider the difference between sitting behind a desk and talking with a fellow employee versus sitting next to one another at a small table. The former implies that we have directives to hand down, whereas the latter implies that there is teamwork to accomplish.

And given that food and drink are often a nice distraction, offering coffee, bottled water, or some munchies is often a welcoming sign. For example, our supervisor conducts our annual reviews in late November or early December, and she always has a small gift that she gives each one of us during the meeting. The fact that we can count on getting a special goody bag gives us something to look forward to in heading to that meeting, and though I'm sure she doesn't look at it this way, it's a wise strategic move on her part. Every bit of positive feelings we can elicit in the people we review is a good thing and will help the conversation be that much more comfortable.

To begin the conversation, we may want to start by reviewing the evaluation process and going over the agenda for the meeting. This is a great opportunity to set the stage for a mutually beneficial conversation by mentioning how much we personally stand to gain from this process as we learn from the work styles of our employees.

One of the top reasons that performance appraisal systems fail is the lack of real discussion, so we must frame the conversation from the start as one that we expect will be a beneficial dialogue. Nothing communicates this message more than our acknowledgement that we too learn and grow from the process. The most effective performance appraisals include an opportunity for two-way communication. That is, participation should be invited, rather than the employee sitting and passively listening. Though we have an agenda, we should split the talking 50/50 with employees being evaluated, using their comments to guide the discussion.

The use of self-appraisals has increased, and they too may provide a great opportunity for the employee to start talking during the performance appraisal interview. A simple question such as, "How do you think your work year has gone?" may prompt input, and it can be followed up with questions such as, "What would you identify as the highlights of your performance?" and "Where would you say you need to grow as an employee at our company?"

At times, self-appraisals lack objectivity on the part of employees and are somewhat overinflated and more positive in nature. Still, they may provide an excellent point of reference for opening the discussion of the employee's performance. If we are lucky enough, the employee will have identified some of our points of discussion during the self-appraisal, and we can naturally transition into them. Regardless of our fortune in this, it is often best to begin with some positive comments, move to our suggestions for improvement, and then end with a few positive summary comments. This agenda begins and ends our conversation on an optimistic note.

When communicating appreciation for the things employees do well or strengths they have, we need to be specific. "Thanks for all you do" is so vague as to almost achieve the opposite effect because it may communicate that we cannot think of anything specific to compliment them on or that we don't know them well enough to even be aware of the things they do. Additionally, if the goal of the performance appraisal is to encourage good behavior, then we need to point out specifically what good behavior looks like so they can endeavor to repeat it.

Because people may not remember numerous items from a list given to them verbally, especially if they feel anxious (for instance, during a performance review), a good rule of thumb is to offer two or three positive comments and two or three negative comments. Perhaps the best advice for providing constructive feedback lies in knowing how to prioritize and even minimize the amount of information. Practically speaking, if we look over employees' specific achievements and struggles from the past year, we may want to put them into broad categories so that we can have two or three main positive and negative comments, each with specific instances for support.

For example, let's say Erin turned in eight out of 20 reports late, yet those reports were always thorough and accurate. Let's also say that she arrived to work late on a fairly regular basis. We would have the general comment to make that one of her strengths is attention to detail, with her accuracy and care in constructing the reports as the concrete example we would offer. When highlighting her strengths, we can mention what we have learned from her or what we admire about her work habits.

Regarding negative comments, we could make the general observation that she needs to put more effort into timeliness, and as concrete examples, we could use the late reports and tardy work arrivals. During the negative comments discussion, we might have the opportunity to identify with her over a common struggle and offer any insight we have toward overcoming it. At the end of the process, we would have provided her with general comments about good behavior to continue doing—with specific areas to focus on—and bad behavior to adjust—with specific areas to focus on.

Offering two or three positive and two or three negative comments and specific examples to support each one will help keep the conversation on track and prevent us from descending into a laundry list of problems. This approach in turn will aid

DID YOU KNOW?

In his book *Everyone Communicates, Few Connect*, John Maxwell reminds us to "express gratitude."[3] Simply put, remember to say thank you—and mean it!

in keeping the conversation from becoming too emotional. Focusing on concrete events that actually happened will cut down on disputes about intentions or other such intangibles.

Especially when talking about an employee's shortcomings, we should use collaborative language instead of directives. Consider the difference between saying, "You need to be a more aggressive sales person," and "How can we work on getting your sales numbers up for the next quarter?" The first example points a finger at employees for something they probably already realize is a problem. It's also loaded with the expectation that the employees will improve the situation on their own, which may be unreasonable. The second example acknowledges the problem but communicates that the employees can count on assistance from the team they are a part of—their company. Using collaborative language is yet another way to diffuse the power dynamic and assure employees that they are not alone.

One last—but essential—component to giving feedback is to tie individuals' performance to the overall goals of the organization. The skill set that employees develop should also be tied to the objectives of their department and the organization. This alignment helps employees see the direct line of sight between their contributions and the success of the organization.

You've Said It...Now What?

Because the appraisal process is designed to be interactive and two-way, we need to ask employees questions throughout the conversation—and then listen to their responses. Part of active listening means listening to employees' words and feelings. The performance evaluation is often a time of high emotions, so listening actively takes practice and a concerted effort not to interrupt. If we are interrupting, we are definitely not listening or learning.

Making the interview interactive also means that we have to welcome questions, and sometimes questions can feel like challenges to our thoughts and comments. We must be able to respond without defensiveness and communicate that we genuinely value open, honest discussion.

This appraisal discussion should lead to an action plan for the future so that employees are not left wondering what they should do with the information they've gained. Based on the positive and negative comments given, we need to describe how employees should move forward.

A final tip for harnessing the power of the performance appraisal and communicating its value is to follow up with employees. If we let a whole year go by without checking in on some of the goals in the employees' action plans, they often won't remember to think about them until a few weeks or days before their next review. The very act of having a brief chat with employees' about one of their goals says to them, "I care about your progress as an employee, and I'm a believer in the power of the appraisal system."

Additionally, setting up "check-ins" halfway through the year can serve as an informal performance appraisal. These can help keep both our employees and us apprised of their progress toward their goals, and it has the added bonus of opening up the dialogue ahead of time to help us both avoid surprises. We know that the best appraisal is one that is not a surprise!

If we follow these communication tips for preparing, conducting, and ending the performance appraisal, we will have a much better chance of making the appraisal process beneficial for the company, the employees, and often even ourselves.

Chapter 8

The Problem Employee (and the Employee with a Problem)

Dealing with problem employees is not a pleasant task. Unfortunately, the cost of *not* dealing with problem employees skyrockets with every week that passes. Mishandling or failing to address these problems incurs both direct and indirect costs for the employee involved, the organization as a whole, and those other employees who choose to leave a toxic situation where problems go unaddressed. These costs include lawsuits, turnover, poor morale, and lost productivity.

IN ACTION

Delivering effective, sensitive communication with a problem employee requires mutual respect and effective conflict management—both subcompetencies of relationship management, as identified by SHRM's Competency Model.[1] Also noteworthy is proactivity. A failure to proactively address the problem employee may create even more challenges for an organization.

Generally, problem employees may be divided into three major categories: performance-related, behavioral, or personal problems. These problems encompass a wide range, from a failure to meet the standards of performance, to insubordination, to alcohol abuse, to inappropriate personal hygiene.

The best practice for dealing with problem employees is prevention—that is, ensuring that all employees know what is expected of them. And this starts with clear and consistent communication from day one. The employee handbook, orientation sessions, and the performance appraisal system are all integral elements in communicating the organization's expectations for employees. However, even with the best communication of expectations, a few employees will still struggle to meet expectations for one reason or another. For them, the best practice for dealing with the problem is still prevention. That is, we want to prevent the problem from continuing or worsening. To do this, we rely on progressive discipline.

Progressive Discipline

In this approach, the objective is more positive in nature than punitive. A progressive approach is used to provide an opportunity to correct problems at each step, avoiding a costly termination when an employee might be salvaged. In other words, progressive discipline could be a misnomer because it is used to encourage behavior changes rather than punish people who are out of line. The stages of progressive discipline begin with a verbal warning, proceed to a written warning, and end in termination. Specific actions and time frames are outlined with the first two stages.

Sometimes, the problems employees cause come from personal issues outside the workplace, such as substance abuse, marital issues, financial crises, or a sudden tragedy; other times, the problems stem from maladjustments within the workplace, such as friction between co-workers, improper job fit, or unrealistic expectations.

Handling these situations is like handling cases of old dynamite: They are fragile, potentially volatile, and can explode in our faces, hurting us, our co-workers, and our company. A full treatment of this topic would include strategies for documenting evidence, specific measures for each step of the process, warning flags for violence, and many other items; however, this is a book about effective communication strategies, so we will focus our attention on how to talk with employees having problems at work—either because they're causing them (they *are* the problem) or because they're bringing the problems to work with them (they *have* problems).

A Word about Evidence

Even though we will focus on communication, we must take a moment to discuss documentation; without documentation, effective communication will not occur. When we talk with employees about their personal problems or performance-related problems, our main tool is concrete evidence. We cannot simply say,

DID YOU KNOW?

"Most performance problems can be resolved through early and effective communication between an employer and the employee. The employees may not even be aware of the change in their performance. Regardless, when an employee's performance first starts to slip, they are more likely to be open to discussing what needs to be done to improve performance. Working with poor performers earlier means employers can help employees improve without the negative consequences of threatening their jobs or taking other disciplinary action."[2]

—*National Federation of Independent Business*

"George, you've been a bit off lately," and expect George to agree with us or even know what we're talking about.

As soon as we notice a potentially problematic issue or behavior occurring in the workplace, we need to write it down and file it as evidence. Too often, by the time we notice the problem and begin to get annoyed by it, we have missed a crucial window during which we could have been documenting the behavior so that we could've had a productive conversation about the problem.

At first, such attention might seem like the actions of a person who is always looking to catch an employee doing something wrong; however, this is not the case. In fact, the opposite is true. These are the actions of vigilant supervisors who want to document both good and bad behavior, so they can give useful and formative feedback for the good of their employees. As mentioned in Chapter 7 on performance appraisals, we need to get into the habit of regularly collecting information about our employees.

This practice also protects employees from supervisors making snap judgments based on a singular occurrence. For example, we may be stressed out by a deadline on the same day that Jim submits a late report. But because we have no record of his ever having had submitted a late report before, we'll hesitate before accusing him of *always* being behind schedule. Collecting evidence enables us to make informed decisions about our employees. It helps us see if a problematic action on one day of the week is symptomatic of a broader trend of downward behavior, or just an aberration because an employee was having a bad day.

As well, if we notice that we've recently added

a few observations of negative behavior to an employee's folder, we'll know we need to have a conversation with that employee soon so that we don't let the problems fester and grow. Part of dealing effectively with struggling employees is addressing problems quickly, before any irreversible damage occurs. Practically speaking, saving employees is always more cost-effective than terminating them and having to look for new ones.

Evidence also protects us. If we have a pile of evidence that speaks to an employee's problematic behavior, she will have a much more difficult time accusing us of partiality. In the long run, the evidence will increase the likelihood of her listening to us (because she's staring at facts, not subjective and unsubstantiated claims) and decrease the likelihood of us landing in court.

So document like your life depends on it. It does.

Charging into the Fray

Okay, now to the point. We document so that we can have productive discussions with our employees, and our main job in handling problems with employees is to address problems directly, listen carefully, discuss solutions, set goals, summarize accurately, review expectations, and then check in regularly.

Many of us are not fans of conflict, so addressing a problem directly is tough for us. We might have documented employees' behavior diligently and noticed a downward trend with one of them, but the idea of directly addressing the problem with the employee turns our stomachs a little.

The underlying philosophy behind "progressive discipline"—the notion that we must address problems quickly and in stages—is that if we talk to our employees quickly enough, when they *start* to struggle, then we improve our chances of saving them. Many times, we think of addressing a problem with an employee as a punitive action, but if we keep the progressive discipline philosophy in mind, addressing problems will be a salvaging action—an attempt to rescue employees from behavior that will hurt them in the long term.

With this in mind, the sooner we address an issue and the more clearly we can point out the problem, the better. Addressing an issue clearly requires a specific kind of communication. For starters, we should set up a private meeting with the individual and let the employee know that the meeting will address a concern we have about the employee's behavior.

At the beginning of the meeting, our primary role is to directly point out the behavior in question and why it is a problem. If we have been documenting the employee's performance, pointing out the behavior will be a matter of opening our notes and saying something like the following:

> On July 12, you forwarded an inappropriate e-mail to your business team, which you said was an accident because you hit the wrong button on your computer. On July 23, you posted an inappropriate picture on the bulletin board of your cubicle, which I asked you to take down. You took it down and said you didn't realize it would offend anyone. Yesterday—August 3—in the lunch room, you told a loud joke that was racially insensitive. Ron pointed this out to you, but you said you didn't mean for it to be taken that way.

Beginning with concrete, indisputable actions sets the foundation for the case from which all subsequent discussion proceeds. Based on the facts, we are able to make a logical inference: "These actions are characteristic of a person who is insensitive to other cultures, races, and genders." We must directly state the heart of the problem that needs to be corrected without mincing words.

If we dance around the issue by saying, "Some people are starting to feel that you might not be aware that your actions seem a little insensitive," the employee is likely to sense the hesitancy and try to argue. "Some people," "might not be," and "seem a little" are all verbal cues of insecurity and hesitancy. Once we decide that a verbal warning is necessary, we should have no sense of hesitancy or wavering in our language.

Being firm yet positive and hopeful that change can occur is why we would say, "These actions are characteristic of a person who is insensitive." The actions *are* characteristics of insensitivity—the actions the employee engaged in were insensitive; however, when we say they are characteristic of a *person* who is insensitive, we offer the employee the chance to choose to act differently. Essentially, the statement allows the employee to see that continued actions in this vein will solidify him as a person who is racially and culturally insensitive, but if he changes his ways, he can distance himself from people who exhibit those kinds of behaviors and get labeled "insensitive."

Once we identify the problem, our next move is to briefly connect the problem with the overall goals of the company. The employee probably recognizes how his problematic behavior is out of line with the goals of the company, but we need to be sure that no misunderstandings occur. Stating the issue clearly is simply a matter of identifying the primary ways the behavior runs counter to the expectations expressed in the employee handbook or other company-published policies: "Section 8 in the handbook addresses employee interactions, and it states that 'employees shall not initiate discussions, send e-mails, or otherwise engage in activity that is offensive to people of another race, class, culture, gender, or sexual preference.' All three of your documented behaviors have violated this expectation." We may—and perhaps even *should*—read straight from the handbook to emphasize this point.

As the previous example illustrates, addressing a problem directly does not require wordiness, nor is wordiness helpful. The last thing we want to do is air a laundry list of offenses, which may sound more like an attack than a productive, forward-looking meeting.

Once we state the problem, we need to let the employee respond. If we tell employees the problems and what they need to do differently, and then let them return to work, we will miss important pieces of the puzzle. Some employees perform poorly because they misunderstand our expectations, some because they haven't been properly trained or prepared for the role they're in, and still others because of personal struggles outside the workplace. Letting our employees respond to the problem we point out shows them that we care about them as people and don't view them as just a cog in the machine. Additionally, we may find out information that will enable us to better address the problem at its root, instead of pushing it underground only to have it resurface again later.

In the example given earlier, we might simply ask the employee, "Does this make sense to you?" or "Do you have any questions about this?" A general and somewhat open question will allow the employee to respond in a variety of ways to the direct problem addressed. An employee might say, "I didn't know I was making people feel this way" or "No, it doesn't make any sense at all.

I think it's ridiculous that people are so sensitive and make such a big deal out of something that was just a joke." Although we would like to hope otherwise, the reality is that the latter option is the more likely response, so we need to have a firm and simple restatement of the problem ready. If we are particularly nervous about how a conversation like this might go, we may want to role-play the situation with someone, such as our manager or a fellow supervisor, who is trustworthy and already knows about the situation.

Asking questions such as the ones above leads well into discussing a solution with the employee. "What can we do to make sure this doesn't happen anymore?" is a classic way of urging employees to think about the problem and some realistic solutions that will work for them. It also shows employees that we do not simply issue directives. Because we are clearly in the power seat in the meeting, we should offer assistance to the employee (for example, "What can I do to help you get back on track?"). We can also ask what kinds of goals should be set to remind employees to be working on the issue and to be guarding against the problem recurring in the upcoming weeks.

Before beginning a meeting to discuss poor performance, we should have some ideas for resolving the problem. During the meeting, we should also listen to employees' ideas so that we may arrive at satisfactory solutions together. We should conclude the conversation with an accurate summary of the discussion to make sure that both parties agree and that expectations have been clearly delivered. Summarizing the main events of the conversation should include a brief statement of the problem, any relevant new information from the employee, what actions the employee will take to correct the

DID YOU KNOW?

"When conversation becomes dialogue, shared understanding emerges and mutual learning takes place."[4]

—Lois J. Zachary

problem, what (if any) actions we will take to assist the employee in his or her endeavors, and the reasonable time line and goals the employee has agreed to.

In addition to reminding the employee about the conversation, this summary also serves as an official statement of the regular feedback the employee may expect to receive regarding the problem. Setting a time line and goals relating to resolving the issue communicates to the employee that we're not going to push the employee out our door and expect things to magically get better. Instead, we acknowledge that reform will be a process and we'll be available to encourage the employee through the various stages of that process.

Delivering the Written Warning

In the event that the problem persists or worsens, the next step would be to file a formal, written warning to provide an employee with the second opportunity to address the problem he or she faces. Although the warning is written, we still have a responsibility to talk with the employee about it.

Once a situation has progressed to the point of the written warning, more dramatic language is needed. If the verbal warning could be likened to a stop light, the written warning could be likened to the lights, bells, whistles, and guards of a railroad crossing. In other words, our tone during the discussion of the written warning needs to be more severe, and that means our body language and verbal message should be very intentional.

Instead of the more wide-eyed, friendly, "we're-in-this-together-and-I'll-help-however-I-can" facial expression of the verbal warning, we need to change our approach because that message clearly didn't motivate the employee to change his or her behavior. Think about the look you give someone when you say something such as, "Do you think that was the right thing to do?" (when the implied answer is, "Of course it wasn't!"). It often includes raised eyebrows and pursed lips. Raising our eyebrows is a better move than furrowing them, which turns our face into a frown. Our goal is not to make the person feel entirely like a child, but we need them to know from our expression that we are serious and that this will be the final conversation before the exit interview.

Our body language should match the tone of our facial expression. During the verbal warning, we might have sat alongside the employee and leaned toward him or her slightly, suggestive of a more cooperative attitude. During the written warning we may choose to sit up straight in our chair behind our desk to project a cooler tone to the relationship. This is the last stop on the "Train out of town," so it's good for our body language to help the employees see that this is their last chance.

Because the function of this meeting will be to go over the written warning, our main responsibility is to read it to outline all the steps taken up to this point. Our greeting to the employee should be courteously professional, but we should resist the impulse to have an overly friendly greeting in an attempt to soften what is about to happen. We may introduce the warning briefly with a statement such as, "It's company policy that when an employee fails to respond to a verbal warning, the final step in the process is a written warning. I'll read you the warning, and then I'll need you to sign it, verifying that you have heard and understood the warning."

Two things are likely to happen during this encounter: First, employees are likely to argue that change has occurred and that they have made improvements; second, employees are likely to refuse to sign the written warning, fearing that by doing so they are admitting guilt they don't want to own.

Addressing both concerns will be much easier if we've taken some preventive measures. First, if we have been documenting behavior and providing regular feedback after the verbal warning, the written warning should not be a huge surprise. As well, if we have concrete evidence in front of us, in response to the employees' arguments we should simply look down at our evidence, pick a few examples, and state them calmly. Staying calm during the meeting is important because our best chance at diffusing the tension will lie in our ability to stay professional and emotionally detached.

Preparation with regard to employees signing the written warning is about properly framing the need for the signature. Employees must hear and understand that the signature is not an admission of guilt but simply an acknowledgment of having read the document and having met with us.

Even though this meeting should be even more somber than the verbal warning, we should acknowledge to ourselves and to employees that we would still like them to straighten up and be a part of the company. Therefore, we need to have a conversation similar to that of the verbal warning, asking for input on why the employee continues to struggle and on how we can better work toward the goals set during the last meeting. The meeting should end on a positive note, with a reminder that we will be checking in regularly to offer feedback and support.

Every workplace will have its problem employees and its employees who have problems. Our job is to use strategic communication tools to enable those employees to succeed instead of allowing them to fall deeper and deeper into a spiral that will harm them, the people around them, and our company. Helping them will help everyone.

Chapter 9

The Termination

"I'll be back." A classic line from a classic movie. If you read it right, with that flat intonation and accent, you couldn't help picturing Arnold Schwarzenegger with his crew cut and black sunglasses. He was great as "The Terminator," and wouldn't it be great if we could pass that responsibility off onto him at our own workplaces? "Hi Pete, Arnie wants to meet with you tomorrow at 3:30—he said something like (and here you could do the accent) 'Hasta la vista, baby…'—I don't know—you'll have to talk to him." Just like that, one of our most stressful encounters would no longer be our responsibility.

Unfortunately for us, Mr. Schwarzenegger will probably not be our in-house terminator anytime soon, so in the meantime, we need some strategies for doing the job ourselves. First, a few comments on preparation: Preparation is essential for a termination interview, or dismissal meeting. Our initial step in preparing is having a safety net in place. All managers and supervisors involved should know when and where the termination meeting will take place so that we will have a cross-company slice of people who know about the situation. Security should be notified in advance, and the legal department (or outside counsel) should be consulted before the meeting.

Even the timing of the interview should be carefully planned. We recommend holding the termination interview on a Monday or Tuesday afternoon. Fewer people are generally in the office during the mid- to late-afternoon hours, which may diminish some of the embarrassment for the employee, and holding the interview early in the week provides the separated employee with an opportunity to immediately begin searching for another job. A Friday interview often leaves the terminated employee simmering over the weekend with no opportunity for taking action to begin the new job search. We should avoid times such as right before a holiday or vacation for the employee.

A private setting is also preferred. A closed office with a door is best so that we can avoid having others looking in on such an emotional exchange. The location should be neutral and definitely on-site.

BBB—But Nope, Not the Better Business Bureau

If the verbal warnings that come with progressive discipline give us a stomach ache, then the termination interview gives us a full-body ache! In fact, research reports that a manager's likelihood of having a heart attack doubles during the week after the termination interview.[1] To avoid that outcome, we need to ease the accompanying stress and tension. If we followed the steps outlined in Chapter 8, we will feel that we have done all we could to help the employee avoid this termination; thus we may avoid any lingering feelings of personal responsibility. As well, having a concrete communication strategy that enables us to feel prepared for the interview is crucial. Our recommendation is to remember the three Bs—like the Better Business Bureau—but for terminations: staying focused on Business, keeping it Brief, and remaining Brave.

When it comes time to let a person go, we must communicate the matter as a business decision, not a personal one. This is critical so that we avoid our company or us winding up in court because the terminated employee felt that we held a personal grudge against him or her. Staying focused on the business case for the decision and saying a sentence such as, "Unfortunately, there hasn't been any improvement in your work performance, so we have to terminate you," communicates that the termination is about job performance, not personal preference. Additionally, phrasing it in this manner points out the problem without unnecessarily pointing a finger in the face of the person being fired. "There hasn't been any improvement in your work performance" is much less accusatory than "You haven't performed any better at work."

IN ACTION

The termination requires a high level of ethical practice in maintaining confidentiality and exhibiting professionalism. Terminating an employee also requires that we maintain objectivity throughout the process, for the good of the employee, the company, and ourselves. (Objectivity is a subcompetency of the Critical Evaluation competency as identified by SHRM's Competency Model.[2])

Because people respond differently when facing such news, we need to follow "There hasn't been any improvement in your work performance" with a few sentences about the documented evidence that we've collected along the route to this terminus: "As you know, a verbal warning was issued to you on January 15, which was then followed by a written warning on March 21. Since the beginning of April, there have been two more instances of insubordination, which has left us no other course of action." Offering concrete evidence will lessen the likelihood that the employee will argue with us about the decision, and having thorough documentation of the case is imperative.

In addition to keeping the conversation focused on business, the conversation should also be brief. We do not need to berate employees with numerous examples of their poor performance, and doing so is likely to cause an argument. After informing employees of the termination decision, we should inform them of any additional information they will need, such as severance information, vacation pay, or benefits details. We should also provide this information in a letter because the employee may forget what was said during this highly emotional exchange.

Because we need to keep the session brief, we should have the information somewhat rehearsed so that we can say it quickly without bumbling around. The final statement to make is to explain the employee's next step and identify his or her contact person, which is usually us.

The third "B"—remaining brave—is about what sometimes happens in our hearts during a termination interview. We might go into the interview with objectivity and resolution, but once we see that big tear roll down her face or his chin start to quiver, our own emotions get stirred, and we have difficulty staying on task. Empathizing in our hearts with these people is okay—and probably healthy. The trouble is that if the emotion works its way into our heads and then out through our lips, we often wind up saying things we do not mean or cannot stand by.

Being brave during the termination interview is about staying true to the facts of the case and not apologizing for the organization. We may be tempted to do so to ease the person's mind; however, doing anything other than plainly stating the facts of the case is dangerous and irresponsible to us and our organization.

As the news sinks in with the employee, he or she may have questions for us. We should remain confident and courteous, answering questions honestly and respectfully, even as the employee may become increasingly disgruntled. (Document such behavior, too, in the event legal action is taken.) As quickly as possible, we should end the meeting and communicate that we're available for additional follow-up and questions, should the employee have any.

Staying focused on business, keeping the conversation brief, and remaining brave will enable us to safely navigate the termination interview; however, our job is not over: The final bridge to cross is notifying others of the termination.

Whenever one employee is let go, other employees may feel endangered, so we should briefly and clearly communicate with others about the termination. Additionally, the terminated person's workload will likely have to be absorbed by others in the organization, so they'll need to know about the changes.

One strategic way to break the news to other staff is to simply say, "John is no longer with us, which means his workload will need to be redistributed." A statement like this one does not tell employees that John was fired, and it therefore protects his privacy. If the employee has been a noticeable problem employee, at least some of the story will be obvious to his or her colleagues; however, if someone asks for details, the best response is, "Out of respect for John's privacy, I'm not at liberty to discuss his personal circumstances." Naturally, if employees have concerns about additional terminations, we need to put their fears at ease (unless there really is cause for concern).

If One Is Bad, How Should We Handle a Group of Them?

In some cases, we find ourselves delivering bad news to not just one employee but to many because of a company restructuring or downsizing. To terminate one employee because he or she is performing poorly is one thing, but to terminate a whole group of employees because of a decision handed down from the C-suite is another. In the first instance, the employee has brought it on himself or herself, whereas in the second, the matter was entirely out of the employees' control. Communicating this kind of sensitive information takes tact and honesty.

The foundation for an effective downsizing effort is to communicate early and often. Open, honest communication that is continuous and two-way will set a tone of transparency that employees will appreciate. Naturally, employees will appreciate being told as early as possible, and the main job we have is to present the business case for the layoffs. Presenting the case so that employees see that the layoff decisions were fair and impartial—coupled with as much advance notice as we can give them—increases the likelihood of their accepting the information.

We should avoid casting the company as the victim: "We were hard-pressed on all sides...we didn't know what to do. It was almost certain we were going to have to shut down the whole operation...and then we realized laying off 1,300 employees would save us! We could stay in business if we just sacrificed the jobs of 1,300 people!" The company is not the victim—the people losing their jobs are the victims, so our message should be honest and respectful.

Throughout the layoff process, employees need us to communicate two key things to them: trustworthiness and empathy. Both of these messages come from verbal and nonverbal behavior. To communicate trustworthiness, we need to be as honest and as clear as we can be about the issues, taking care not to dodge topics without giving straightforward answers. If we have been told that some topics are off-limits, the best way for us to maintain our trustworthiness is to tell employees who ask about those topics, "I'm sorry, I've been told that this information needs to be kept private. As soon as I'm able to share it, I will." Then we need to follow up on those promises.

Additionally, making eye contact with employees will aid the communication process. Sending the message that we are telling the truth about the information we're privy to will require more personal eye contact throughout our audience. This will enable each individual to understand that although we dislike delivering the information, we're making sustained eye contact because we're not hiding information from them.

Because these kinds of meetings are likely to elicit lots of questions, we need to come prepared, having thought through all the different concerns and questions that might be asked. As well, top managers should participate so that they can both show their support and answer critical questions. It will take thoughtful preparation to communicate the specific layoff policy to all those affected and to provide employees with ample opportunity to have their questions answered.

Communication should include multiple channels. Regular "town hall"-style meetings can provide the open communication that builds loyalty and trust. Some companies supplement these meetings with newsletters devoted to the downsizing effort.

The use of the bunker mentality (running in to hide under our desks), results in an overworked rumor mill. When people lack information, they tend to think the worst. Contempt and disloyalty often result when employees are not kept apprised of the process. They begin to lose trust in human resources and in management—with good reason. When employees are treated with openness, trust, and loyalty, they respond with the same.

Communicating empathy to employees means acknowledging the emotional nature of the process instead of trying to ignore it. We should communicate how very sorry we are to have to bring such hard news to them. Additionally, we should acknowledge that although we are presenting a business case for the layoffs and no one will be personally targeted, losing one's job is a very personal and potentially devastating event that we need to be sensitive to.

Nonverbal empathy is just as important as verbal empathy. In fact, if our nonverbal actions don't match our words, our trustworthiness is likely to erode. Showing emotion and avoiding seeming aloof communicate that we acknowledge the pain employees feel during the process. We may convey emotion with something as simple as a touch on the elbow or shoulder, but people often read it in our eyes. Taking the time to address people's concerns one-on-one or in small groups affords moments of connection in which people know we are conscious of their concerns.

The Layoff Interview

By the time the day of the actual layoff news comes, if we have actively prepared as recommended in the previous section, we will be able to notify the people who have been laid off and conduct the difficult conversations. We will be a familiar, sympathetic, and trustworthy face, tasked with breaking the bad news. As with any termination interview, we'll want to keep it brief and to the point, given that nothing we can say will help the matter.

The importance of keeping the discussion brief doesn't mean that we can abdicate responsibility and communicate the news via e-mail, as one well-known company did, to the injury of its reputation. Instead, we should have a face-to-face conversation with individuals. This in-person communication—taking a moment to sit down and spend some time with the affected employees— also provides the company with the opportunity to remind employees that we don't view them as just numbers. This message will hopefully minimize the likelihood of a disgruntled employee causing a public relations nightmare for us. If we treat each of the employees with dignity and respect as they leave, they are less likely to go into the community or onto Facebook to rant about what a horrible company we run.

Small details make all the difference in communicating respect and fairness for our laid-off employees. Although a full-fledged outplacement firm does not need to be offered, employees may be provided with workshops in resume preparation, and when appropriate, letters of recommendation may be offered. Some companies have gone so far as to contact their competitors on behalf of their laid-off employees. We might even offer to stay late to help them pack their personal belongings. Because we are one of the last faces of the company that these employees will see, we have an opportunity to create in them the feeling that the company does still care about them. This is yet another opportunity for the company to do well by the community.

The exit interview also presents us with an opportunity to mine for gold. Also referred to as the separation interview, it provides us with the chance to ask critical questions of those individuals who are separating from the organization—either voluntarily or involuntarily. To better manage the cost of hiring, we should understand as many of the reasons for attrition as possible. Exit interviews give us a chance to reduce our turnover costs because the

DID YOU KNOW?

According to Challenger, Gray & Christmas' *2011 Year-End Job Cut Report & Economic Outlook,* the number one reason for layoffs in 2011 was restructuring.[3]

feedback helps us correct HR practices within our control.

We do, however, need to set the stage to encourage candor. As the HR professional, we were probably not the employee's direct supervisor, so we may be more likely to create an environment in which employees feel comfortable sharing more insights. A neutral location can help create this environment.

We might ask exiting employees what they enjoyed and did not enjoy about their job. Then we might lead into a more difficult question about what they might have changed or what they thought of their supervisor. We also want to find out where the employees are going—and why. In the case of voluntary separations, we want to understand why they are leaving (especially if they are high-potential candidates whom we wanted to retain). Probing for information on whether their expectations concerning the job and the company were met may be helpful. Starting with general questions and then working up to the more specific, sensitive questions is also often an effective approach.

The exit interview provides us with an opportunity to track trends. We may gain unexpected insights, such as possible equal employment opportunity (EEO) concerns (more women and minorities leaving from certain departments, for example), news that employees are voluntarily resigning from the same positions (perhaps highlighting a lack of training for or a lack of career track from that position), or compensation and benefits matters. We are looking for trends. For example, an inordinate number of new employees leaving during the probationary period may signal a number of problems, including poor hiring practices and a failure to use realistic job previews. Exit interviews yield valuable learning opportunities that we should take advantage of and then disseminate what we learn to the proper departments.

Since Arnold Schwarzenegger is not available to conduct our termination interviews for us, we will have to settle for knowing that preparing effectively will minimize our stress and enable us to communicate in a way that lessens the pain for the employee as well.

Chapter 10

Getting Buy-In from Peers: Persuasive Lateral Conversations

Communication flows in three directions (up, down, and sideways), but we tend to give less attention to the sideways flow. Yet the very nature of collaborative relationships depends on this communication flow. HR departments are specifically positioned to share information with other departments and to serve as business partners, highlighting the critical need for lateral communication.

With flatter organizational structures today, a failure to communicate effectively across positions and between departments may result in little or no coordination between functions. The temptation in the past has been to hoard information and expertise as the basis of power; however, the real power comes from sharing the information! Becoming a direct channel of communication also opens the door to establishing relationships, which is so vital to human resources. The traditional staff relationship between the HR department and the rest of the organization depends on these open, direct channels of communication. To serve as strategic business partners, human resources must excel in lateral communication.

IN ACTION

SHRM's Competency Model defines organizational leadership and navigation as "the ability to direct initiatives and processes within the organization with agility and to gain buy-in from stakeholders."[1] Promoting consensus is a critical part of the HR professional's role. Gaining buy-in requires cultural effectiveness and openness to diversity, as well as courage, professionalism, and ethical practice.

The benefit of sharing information between peers is that it can be a helpful means of resolving conflict, facilitating cooperation, coordinating work, solving problems, and providing assistance. As an HR professional, the ability to be effective in the job depends on mastering the art of lateral communication. Promoting consensus is a critical part of the HR professional's role.

When engaging in downward communication, position power may be used to "persuade" others. That is, our authority (inherent in the position) may be used to encourage others to do what we need them to do. However, in lateral communication, personal power is required because everyone is equal in position power.

Though persuasion might be considered a form of manipulation (in that we are influencing others to do what we want them to do), when used effectively it still leaves the other individual free to choose to comply or not. Persuasion is more about encouraging others to accept our point rather than about dictating or directing them in what they must do.

Prepare Now: Developing a Base for Persuading

The foundation for effectively persuading others is credibility. When we have earned the trust and confidence of others, we are more likely to be successful persuading them. Ironically then, the work of persuading begins before we actually have anyone to persuade! We must first gain credibility, and we do so by connecting with people in ways that enable them to like us and trust us.

One of Robert Cialdini's laws of persuasion is the law of liking.[3] Personal charisma, likeability, or emotional intelligence is easy enough to build—though many people don't pay particular attention to it. Building our likeability in turn builds our personal power and lays the groundwork for us to use our persuasive abilities when needed. Some people resist an argument simply on the basis of who is presenting the information, but we are more likely to avoid this barrier if we become known as likeable individuals. The more likeable we are, the more likely we are to be persuasive.

Pick Me! Pick Me!—How Do We Get People to Like Us?

Although likeability may sound like something magical that we either have or don't have, we can intentionally engage in behaviors that increase our likeability. For example, friendliness, encouragement, sensitivity, humor, humility, and genuineness are all elements that contribute to a person's likeability. The last item in the list—genuineness—must characterize all the other items for them to seem authentic. For instance, if I walk down the hallway and greet a co-worker with a forced smile and fake enthusiasm, the co-worker will feel my lack of authenticity, and my actions will not have increased my likeability at all. (They may have even decreased it.)

Each day, we can do simple things around our office that will build our likeability. Greeting people with a real smile and a kind word is an easy way to start, and it may become a habit. The rest of the items on the list require more attentiveness on our part. To become a good encourager entails keeping track of people's projects and contributions and then taking the time to genuinely tell them that we noticed something they did well. And of course, genuine encouragement depends on specific knowledge of what exactly a person has accomplished. Otherwise, our comments may sound vague and not authentic.

Sensitivity should not be misconstrued as being teary or dramatic. Being appropriately sensitive in the workplace means being compassionate when we hear about our co-workers' struggles, but it's even broader than that and encompasses the breadth of treating our co-workers the way they would like to be treated. That kind of treatment means talking to them as peers and teammates instead of in condescending or bossy tones. It also means not unnecessarily discussing issues that make them uncomfortable or angry.

Humor and humility can go together, although this pairing might not be immediately intuitive. Humor is often a tricky character trait to manage because people's humor preferences vary so widely; however, the goal with a sense of humor isn't to be the side-splitting, stand-up comic of the office—it's simply to have a sense of humor. Sometimes, likeable people are not the ones delivering the one-liners but the ones enjoying them. People like when others laugh at their jokes. Additionally, people like when we can easily laugh at ourselves, without becoming defensive; this is where humility can often be paired with humor. To recount a funny moment of panic or error shows that we don't take ourselves too seriously and therefore are less likely to be a hassle to work with.

In connection with an ability to tell funny stories about ourselves, we show humility by admitting when we make mistakes. Owning up to a blunder and apologizing for it shows our colleagues that we recognize our imperfections. And, boy, is it nice to work with people who know they aren't perfect!

The same goes for the way we talk about our lives. If we talk about everything we do and everything that happens in our lives as if it were all tinged with gold, we create a superhuman impression of ourselves. (If your Facebook status has ever read, "No lines at Disney!" consider yourself guilty.) Instead, we should allow ourselves to seem like ordinary people who struggle with the same issues as everyone else: raising kids, responding to kooky neighbors, and being kindhearted in all situations. As well, promoting the good work of others instead of talking only about our own achievements is another great way to increase our likeability factor through humility.

In addition to simply being likeable, we need to be trustworthy for our co-workers to consider us credible. As with likeability, we can be intentional about building our sense of trustworthiness. Trustworthiness entails being knowledgeable, impartial, honest, confidential, and consistent. Essentially, we need to be trustworthy on two levels—on a work level and on a relational level.

As employees, we build trustworthiness by meeting deadlines, submitting quality work, and developing relevant expertise in our field. When we prove that we know what we're talking about and that we do our jobs well, our co-workers are much more likely to trust and value our opinions. In addition, we need to show that our judgment is not tainted by personal motives or preferences. Other employees need to see that we are impartial and consistent in the way we make decisions and how we accomplish tasks.

This kind of trustworthiness is valuable, but we can magnify our trustworthiness twofold by being relationally trustworthy. Even if we're great employees, if we are not relationally safe, our co-workers won't really trust us. Being relationally safe means that when we discover something negative about a fellow employee or when we are told something private, we take care to keep the information confidential. When co-workers hear us telling stories about other co-workers, they'll assume that they will be treated the same way, if they give us the chance. Relational trustworthiness is also about maintaining a consistent attitude and demeanor. No one feels comfortable around a volatile personality that can go off at any moment. It deteriorates trustworthiness, and overall, kills our credibility.

If we intentionally invest energy into building our likeability and trustworthiness so that we're viewed as a credible source of information and resourcefulness, we are much more likely to be successful when the time comes to secure peer buy-in for an idea or initiative.

Bring a Big Stick? Maybe...(If There's a Big Carrot on One End)

When the need arises to gain buy-in from peers, having our ideas heard will not take much convincing if we've already built a base of credibility. But credibility is not the golden key to successful persuasion. We also have to remember that the best sales people are highly skilled at putting themselves in the shoes of the people they are persuading.

Two important actions will increase our ability to persuade our peers: showing our audience (whoever they may be) that we share similar values and that we have thought carefully about their context and what will realistically benefit them.

Showing our audience that we share similar values is about highlighting the things we agree on. For example, if we are pushing for a change to the payroll system from every other Friday to the first and fifteenth of the month, we are likely to agree at least in part with those co-workers who initially oppose our idea. We probably both agree on the importance of providing compensation to employees in a way that best addresses their needs and that fits our company's cash flow. We might disagree on the best method to carry out that goal, but drawing attention to what we agree on is nonetheless a beneficial persuasive move.

According to Guy Kawasaki, "The best negotiators spend 40% of their preparation time finding shared interests with the other party."[5] Pointing out our similarities helps remind the person with whom we're arguing that we are thoughtful and reasonable people, a fact that occasionally gets forgotten once a discussion begins. Moreover, knowing that we share values may help our co-workers concede our points.

Practically speaking, one subtle strategy to communicate shared values is to appear more similar to our co-workers through body language and speaking style. Although we wouldn't want to imitate their every move, mirroring their movements and style may convey our similarities nonverbally, thereby making them more likely to be persuaded. In addition, using "we" instead of "I" similarly communicates solidarity and partnership.

We also need to show our audience that we've thought about their needs and desires by communicating empathy. The most persuasive people are the ones who can accurately identify the things their audience values most and highlight how their proposal will address those values in tangible, realistic ways. For example, presuming that all audiences will value money the same way is a false assumption. Some folks will respond more favorably to evidence that a proposal will encourage responsible citizenship, whereas others will respond better to one encouraging more personal freedom. We must do our homework so that we can correctly target and appeal to the core

DID YOU KNOW?

In his book *Power Listening*, Bernard T. Ferrari suggests that we apply the 80/20 rule to communicating: listen 80 percent of the time, and talk 20 percent of the time.[6] Good listening helps improve relationships!

values people hold to.

One of the best ways to know our audience is to listen well. We cannot be prepared to respond well to information, requests, or arguments we have not heard. As Stephen Covey points out, "Seek first to understand, then to be understood."[7] Part of listening well is watching carefully too. For example, if we pay close attention to body language, we will know when a person does not understand—so that we can clarify a point—or does not agree—so that we can offer additional evidence to support our point.

In addition to identifying what will most appeal to other people, we must also conduct our due diligence to know where resistance is likely to emerge. To overcome people's resistance, we have to identify what is meaningful to them. Even better, if we did our homework well enough, we will be able to anticipate their resistance and be ready to respond. Knowing their goals will enable us to better provide a linear, logical progression of ideas addressing their resistance.

During these discussions, we must avoid resorting to condescending language, speaking negatively about other people's ideas, and overloading people with jargon and acronyms. No one likes to be treated like an inferior, and if we use language people don't understand (jargon and acronyms) or have a condescending tone, they are likely to tune us out not because of the quality of our ideas but because of the character of our approach. In addition, anytime we speak degradingly of another person or his or her ideas, we run the risk of someone in the audience knowing that individual or of simply looking mean-spirited or like a bully.

Taking care throughout our work experience to build credibility and know our peers well will enable us to smoothly negotiate the major lateral conversations we face. In turn, we will be able to extend our influence much farther and improve our company.

Chapter 11

Managing Up

How many movies have involved people trying to kill or otherwise seriously harm their bosses? It ranges from Dolly Parton's "9 to 5" to the most recent, "Horrible Bosses." The good news is that you don't have to consider murdering your boss to get ahead, to be heard, or simply to be more effective. As a healthier alternative, we would recommend managing up.

We all manage relationships in multiple directions. These mirror the directions of communication in the organization: that is, we manage relationships with subordinates, superiors, and peers. All three must be managed simultaneously. Unfortunately, many people forget—or don't know how—to manage up.

Managing up is not so much about being good employees for our bosses; it's about asserting ourselves upward. The very term, "managing up," is a seeming paradox because managers are naturally assumed to be telling those under them how to act; however, as HR professionals, we have the unique opportunity to have lots of conversations with people above our pay grade, so we must learn the art of making persuasive recommendations to (in other words, managing) those above us.

When we fail to manage up, we leave untapped potential on the table. That is, we leave opportunities unexplored for ourselves, our subordinates, and even our bosses and company.

Managing upward relationships includes our direct manager, his or her boss, and any other people at higher organizational levels than ourselves. HR professionals must be skilled in managing these relationships. Providing counsel and advice to those at higher organizational levels requires an ability to manage up, and the very nature of many HR roles requires an ability to communicate effectively with those at higher levels.

Jack Welch, former CEO of General Electric, has always advised people to engage in activities that make their managers look good and that help them in their goal achievement.[1] In this way, we become valuable assets to our bosses and our organization. Learning to effectively cultivate and maintain relationships with superiors can become the source of our personal competitive advantage. Managing up extends beyond just managing our own boss; it involves all the relationships we cultivate with those in higher-status positions throughout the organization.

IN ACTION

Serving as a transformational leader, HR professionals must be effective consensus builders—which often means managing up. According to SHRM's Competency Model, organizational leadership means that the HR professional "understands the most effective and efficient way to accomplish tasks within the parameters of organizational hierarchy, processes, systems, and policies."[2]

Managing up is often confused with buttering up. This could not be further from the truth. In fact, using excessive flattery is counterproductive to effectively managing up because it's not authentic and does not develop trust or rapport. This type of behavior is seen by others—and usually by the boss—as manipulative, and managing up is not about manipulating. It's more about creating a win/win/win relationship whereby you, the boss, and the organization all win.

Our relationship with our boss is characterized by mutual dependence. Our manager needs us, and we need him or her. By nature of our boss being our superior, it's tempting to think that all the directives and initiatives should come from him or her, and our task is simply to carry them out faithfully. Though doing what our superiors want is certainly a part of our responsibility, if we allow this to become the entirety of our responsibility, we miss out on many opportunities. Therefore, our responsibility is to actively manage the relationship rather than to passively let it evolve, allowing the boss to drive the entire relationship.

For Starters: Reconnaissance

Managing up begins with awareness. We need to take an inventory of style, strengths, weaknesses, preferences, interests, and dislikes. When our awareness of ourselves and our superiors includes these key items, we will be better able to talk to our bosses the way they hear best.

Knowing our own style and how it compares to our manager's is critical not just to managing up but to success in general in the workplace. For example, if our boss always begins meetings on time and with a brief statement of the items on the agenda, we should not run a meeting he attends by arriving late and opening with, "We're just gonna keep it loosey-goosey today—who wants to talk first?" Style is closely tied to personality types, so figuring out our boss' style of leadership, communication, and living is paramount.

Assessing strengths and weaknesses is similarly important. We need to acknowledge our own limitations as well as those of our manager. In an ideal situation, we would possess strengths in the areas in which our boss is weak and vice versa so that we would complement one another; however, even if this is not the case, knowing both our well-fortified and susceptible areas will enable us to make better decisions.

In assessing our strengths and weaknesses, we must also recognize our approach to authority. Do we assume authority figures are all-knowing? Do we always defer to authority? Do we take a subordinate defensive mode of "you're right/I'm wrong" when dealing with authority figures? Or do we have an innate distrust of authority figures? Do we assume they're "out of touch" or are "know-it-alls"? Whatever our attitude is, we will reveal it in all we do and say, so we must be aware of it and how it will flavor our interactions and perhaps predispose us to certain responses and positions.

Knowing our boss' likes and dislikes helps us avoid inadvertently stepping on a conversational landmine. We can note his or her preferences by listening carefully and observing nonverbal cues. For example, if he sets his jaw and breaks eye contact with us every time we bring up a certain subject, he is signaling that he dislikes that topic. Or if her eyebrows rise and she leans forward and starts talking rapidly, the topic probably interests her. Keeping track of these preferences will help us in the long run.

Ultimately, knowing our boss is about knowing his or her goals and embracing them as our own so that we can help our boss succeed. Part of our job is to make our manager's job easier; we are in a mutually dependent relationship. Managers can shine their spotlight on us and highlight our good work, but the relationship is a two-way street. We wield a great deal of power because we too have the power to make our boss look good—or bad!

To succeed in managing the relationship with our manager, we need to remember the strategic objectives of the firm and how they are aligned with our manager's goals. We can then more strategically share our talents, information, and knowledge to help our boss be more effective. Because our boss' interests take priority, we should take the initiative to jump in and volunteer our assistance or at least ask what we can do to help. In some cases, we might even anticipate our boss' needs. Becoming a strategic thinker helps us anticipate our manager's needs.

Once we know our own style, strengths, and weaknesses, and those of our manager, we can better align them to maximize productivity and harmony.

Upward Communication = Upward Mobilization

Once we've done our homework of scouting out our boss' tendencies and preferences, we can more effectively communicate with him or her. But what, exactly, do we need to intentionally communicate about, and how can we better communicate?

First, the what: In addition to communicating about the tasks of everyday life, we must make time to communicate about problems we face, mistakes we've made, ideas we have, and successes and strengths we've observed in our boss. These are the foursome that we tend to push aside throughout our busy work schedule. Few of us like to talk about problems we're having or the mistakes we've made, and sometimes we feel awkward talking about our own ideas or the ways our boss has impressed us. But talking about things like these separates the great employees from the good ones.

In business, it is safe to say that no one likes surprises—least of all, our boss. Keeping our manager informed and checking in regularly is crucial. Although progress reports and periodic updates are essential, upward communication generally tends to be more guarded; however, trying to hide problems is the worst possible approach. We want to avoid overreacting and running to the boss with every hiccup or glitch, but we have to strike the right balance between taking care of the work we are supposed to be handling and letting our boss know as soon as an unwieldy problem proves unmanageable. If we wait too long—until the problem is out of control and has become a crisis—it will be past the point when we *should* have informed our boss.

Even when we have a problem we know we need to talk to our manager about, no one wants to be known for creating problems for his or her boss. A proactive approach, then, is to offer some solutions alongside the problem. In addition, when we state the problem, we should have some idea of why the problem is occurring and share what actions we have already taken to address it. Classic openings for a discussion might include, "Before you hear it from somebody else" or "It's not as bad as it could have been."

The natural impulse when communicating to a superior about a problem is to pass any responsibility for the problem onto others so that we look better. This practice is counterproductive in managing up. People make mistakes, and trying to appear perfect for managers will show them that we cannot accept responsibility and that we fear failure. If, however, we avoid finger-pointing and instead own up to our mistakes, our boss will see two things: responsibility and resilience—two great leadership qualities.

Just as we need to take a proactive, solution-oriented approach when highlighting problems and admitting mistakes, we also need to be forward-looking in our daily work. We need to ask ourselves what problems our manager (or department or company) is facing and what solutions we might be able to devise. Then we need to share those ideas with our boss. Having a solution-oriented perspective requires timing, assertiveness, and the kind of persuasion we talked about in Chapter 10, but with the tact added by learning our boss' preferences and style.

Once we know managers' preferences and style, pitching ideas to them will include choosing an opportune time and showing how our ideas can further their progress. To avoid throwing ideas at our boss every time we think of one, we should first reflect on his or her main priorities and generate ideas that contribute to those priorities. Presenting ideas to our boss that appeal to his or her core work initiatives will make us more persuasive.

In addition to knowing our boss' vision, preferences, and style, we should also promote our boss in the workplace—complimenting him or her enhances our ability to persuade. Nothing communicates more to managers that we support them than praising their successes and strengths to others. Again, we don't want to act like their lapdog; we simply want to give praise where it's due. Praising our manager to others in the office does not sound like, "Hey, did you hear about how amazing Terry is? Yeah, he crushed that deal with the buyers yesterday—you should have seen it: Pure skill—nobody could touch him." When talking to our boss, praise is not, "Wow, you were better than anyone else could possibly be in this company. Seriously. You should run this company because you have more talent in your little finger than all the people in the chain of command above you."

What distinguishes genuine and effective praise from bragging or fake flattery is sincerity and tact. When we praise our boss—to his or her face or to others—it should first of all flow from a sincere and realistic appreciation of his or her talents. Second, it should fit in the natural flow of conversation so that it doesn't feel forced and therefore not authentic. For example, if a co-worker talks about the deal our boss was involved in closing, we might make a single-sentence comment such as, "I was really impressed with how clearly Terry laid out what the buyers stood to gain from going with us on this deal."

Moreover, when our boss secures these great successes, we should acknowledge them genuinely with the same kind of comment: "I was really impressed with how well you laid out what the buyers stood to gain from going with us on this deal." We need not gush, but we do need to be quick to offer admiration. This is how to proactively manage our relationship with our boss. Communicating about our manager's successes to him or her and others displays our loyalty and respect.

The Information Dump

When we proactively manage our relationships with our superiors, we increase the likelihood that they will turn to us for ideas, and we will inevitably have the opportunity to both deliver information to them and attempt to persuade them.

Delivering information to superiors hinges on accurately identifying the kind of information they most want to hear. Often, even though their requests might seem explicit—"I want you to report on last month's training of the new hires"—considering their motives for asking and their individual roles and goals in the company can help us tailor the information we deliver so that they walk away satisfied. For instance, if our boss asked us to report on last month's training of the new hires, we should immediately ask ourselves why she wants this information. Is she from a particular department and therefore most wants to hear specifically about those new hires? Is she a senior-level HR manager and wants to know how effective the training was or how they responded to a new training tool we recently implemented? Delivering information well begins with identifying the kind of information we are being asked to deliver.

Our other priority in delivering information needs to be striking the right balance between thoroughness and conciseness. We need to clearly say all that needs to be said, and only what needs to be said. In this regard, perhaps we should err on the side of delivering less, while being prepared to deliver more. This approach allows our superiors to ask as many questions as they need, and if we prepared well, we'll be able to answer all their questions well.

Practically speaking, a good way to achieve this delicate balance is to jot down all the details that could be said about the subject on which we're speaking. We can then flesh out all that might be said on the subject and then go back and strategically pull out the three most important things that must be said. From there, we can more specifically develop the critical details that must be said about those three items. In this way, the information we present will drill down into what we see as the heart of the subject, but we can still bring our notes on all the other items that might be of interest to our audience.

The Pitch

If we find ourselves pitching an idea, product, or policy to our superiors, that's a good thing. When we proactively manage our relationships with our superiors, we become much more likely to have the opportunity to convince them of paths we think the company should move down. And knowing our superiors well will pay off when we need to be persuasive.

Persuading is about appealing to the interests of others and about showing them what they stand to gain by adopting our mindset, strategy, or preferred commodity. If we've been studious about learning our boss' goals and preferences, we can recognize the things about our idea, product, or policy that our boss will find exciting. Similarly, we should also quickly recognize the aspects of our idea that our boss will not like. Knowing these two pieces of information is essential to successfully persuading.

For example, let's say we have a great new plan that will increase productivity but will cost the company a good bit of money up front. If we have a boss who is constantly beleaguered by a higher-level boss or by a board focused on cost-cutting, we know we will have a difficult time selling our idea to our boss. Any conversation about our great new plan must begin with persuasive numbers—carefully researching how much money the company is currently losing because of a lack of productivity, how much time and money the company might gain from the increase in productivity, and how likely the company is to realize an increase in productivity.

Regardless of a manager's particular pet peeves, any attempt to motivate action needs to begin by showing how the current course of action is insufficient, move to showing how the proposed course of action will remedy that insufficiency, and end with showing how the proposed course of action will come with tangible benefits. Each phase of this conversation must be tailored to address our boss' priorities and style. Thus, to show that a current course of action is insufficient, we would need to highlight how it falls short of some clear goals our boss has. To show that our proposed course of action will fix that problem, we need to realistically project how our idea addresses the problem at its root and in its entirety. To show that our proposed course of action will come with useful benefits will entail highlighting the ways it will more robustly support our boss' initiatives.

When we're proactive about managing our relationship with our manager and other superiors, we will be able to communicate with them in ways they prefer and set the stage for those sometimes-difficult moments when we need to be persuasive.

DID YOU KNOW?

According to Rick Gilbert, "The rules for presenting to top-level leaders are different."[3] He recommends presenting the bottom line as your first line. Be specific about your reason for being there. Be specific and concise in articulating what you want—and be sure to support your case.

Chapter 12

Special Cases

Admit it: You've daydreamed about being Sherlock Holmes. You've pictured yourself sitting comfortably in a chair, in full possession of a staggering amount of evidence (and intellect), casually answering investigators' questions and blithely leading them to the obvious conclusion you deduced days beforehand.

Okay, so maybe it's not Holmes you've imagined yourself as, but most of us—thanks to TV and movies—have pictured ourselves delivering one of those stirring and convincing orations, after which all doubt as to guilt or innocence has been erased.

Unfortunately, most of us will never even be in the situation where we would have the opportunity to deliver such an address. And for the small percentage of us who do find ourselves in this kind of situation, we're not usually astounding people with our verbal prowess—we're usually, well, pretty jittery.

> **IN ACTION**
>
> A key competency identified in the *SHRM Competency Model* is organizational leadership and navigation. Defined as "the ability to direct initiatives and processes within the organization with agility and to gain buy-in from stakeholders,"[1] strong communication skills are at the heart of these leadership behaviors.

A workplace situation we *are* more likely to find ourselves in is hosting investigatory people, ranging from auditors to compliance officers from the Equal Employment Opportunity Commission (EEO) or the Occupational Safety and Health Administration. The common thread these all share is that they are out-of-the-ordinary occurrences that HR professionals need to be ready to handle nonetheless.

Court Appearances

If ever we are summoned to appear before a court, the most beneficial thing we can do is to prepare well. Because we often have an extended period of time between the events in question and the court appearance, we should thoroughly review all the facts we have documented. Reviewing our documentation several times will enable us to speak from written evidence rather than trying to rely on memories that may have grown fuzzy with time.

When the day of our court appearance comes, we can do a few practical things to help us through it. First, eating healthy, well-balanced meals will help our bodies make it through the potentially long and probably exhausting day. Anytime our bodies experience the rush of nerves likely to occur on an occasion such as appearing in court, they must rely on stored fuel reserves that will only be available if we've eaten nutritious meals leading up to the event.

Another practical move is to dress in comfortable yet conservative business attire. We want to look the part of the professional, but we also need to choose an outfit that will not leave us second-guessing whether it's too low-cut, short, tight, frumpy, or mismatched. Now is not the time to buy a snappy new outfit and then fuss with it throughout the day—now is the time to pick out that comfortable pair of shoes and reliable shirt and suit combo that looks great but makes us feel at ease. Given that we have no idea how long the process will take, we want to dress in a way that will enable us to relax while waiting.

Once we are seated, and an attorney begins to ask us questions, we need to listen closely to the whole question, and then answer only that question. We may have to resist the nervous impulse to rush into answering the question we think the attorney is asking, which could risk our offering information the attorney has not requested. Waiting until the entire question has been asked will enable us to respond appropriately. At times, we'll need to ask for clarification when necessary. Again, our nervous impulse might be to attempt to answer a question we don't understand; however, the much wiser approach is to ask for the question to be rephrased or repeated so that we can better understand what is being asked of us.

Before answering, it's perfectly normal to pause and gather our thoughts. The court isn't looking for rapid-fire answers; it's looking for clearly articulated information that addresses the questions posed. A pause to frame up our answer can help us accomplish this. When answering, we should address the attorney asking the question. General practice is not to address the jury directly unless specifically instructed to do so with a phrase such as, "Please tell the jury...."

Another critical mistake to avoid is sharing more information than is asked for—we can be reprimanded by the court for doing so. Our answers should be straightforward and concrete, avoiding figurative language and metaphors. The court is not looking for poetry; it is looking for facts. Finally, when answering a question, we should admit when we truthfully do not know the answer to a question. The court is looking for honest answers to the questions asked, not conjecture or information we feel *might* be related. While this may seem obvious, it is worth repeating: be truthful.

The image we create is as important as the words we speak. To be viewed as a credible witness, we must pay attention to our body language and tone of voice. We should avoid all the common actions that show we are closed or are hiding something, such as crossing our arms, covering our mouths with our hands, fidgeting in our chair, avoiding eye contact, or mumbling. Instead, we should adjust the microphone to our height, speaking clearly and steadily into it when responding. Our tone should be respectful and polite, without a trace of annoyance or sarcasm. If a question—or even a testimony from another person—surprises us, we should put on our best poker face and avoid rolling our eyes, gasping, or showing any other visible reactions.

When finished presenting our testimony, we should wait for the judge to excuse us. Then we

DID YOU KNOW?

A study published in *Human Resource Development Quarterly* reported that "about half of someone's perception of you as an expert is related to how you carry yourself and convey your message."[2]

can return to our seat and relax, knowing that although we might not have dazzled everyone with our performance, we did our job of supplying honest, professional testimony.

Compliance Visits or Investigations

Hearing our number called when we're playing bingo or clutching a raffle ticket is always fun, but when our number gets drawn for an audit, no one cheers. Companies usually have policies in place for handling these events, and sometimes those policies involve HR professionals. Similarly, the company's receipt of an EEO charge may result in an on-site visit that would involve us. Additionally, if we operate in an industry (or a company) that has a high injury rate or if our facility has had a recent complaint or injury, we should generally be prepared for a possible safety and health inspection.

Most companies have an established response plan that addresses workplace inspections; given that HR professionals must often manage aspects of these visits, we should be familiar with our company policies. Though the specifics of these visits may vary widely, practicing a few general tips will help ensure effective communication.

Because a compliance or investigation visit rarely comes unannounced, we should study the details of the event in question as soon as we know about an upcoming visit. The more familiar we are with the situation, the more useful we will be as a communicator for our company.

Being a communicator *for* our company is an important mindset to have. As representatives of our company, we have an obligation to communicate positively about our company. In some ways,

DID YOU KNOW?

In his article "Body Language Affects First Impressions," Terry Bragg reports that "a first impression is primarily dependent upon your nonverbal signals. To make a favorable first impression, you must use your body language to your advantage."[3]

we are defenders of our company, and the best way we can protect the company is to treat the investigators with politeness and compliance.

Our visit with the investigators begins with a courteous request for credentials. Unless the investigators have already been vetted by security, they will expect this request, and instead of being annoyed by it, they should view it as our company's careful management of the people who come through our buildings. What follows from us should be a careful balance of friendly hospitality and serious discourse. The investigators have a job to do, so we need to be seen as eagerly smoothing the path for them to complete their task, while not seeming overly-chummy.

A "can-do" attitude and promptness will therefore be our best assets. The can-do attitude of providing what the inspectors need will communicate transparency and show them we have nothing to hide. Promptness will also signal this, as it will show them we are not blocking their investigation and that we respect them and value their time and their process. Our attitude may help generate goodwill between our company and the investigators, which is never a bad thing in such circumstances.

As much as we might glamorize the role of someone testifying or acting as an evidence-gatherer, the experience is usually pretty nerve-racking. The key to any situation in which we are facilitating an investigation is being well prepared before the event and then maintaining a positive, helping tone and direct language during it.

Chapter 13

The Everyday Informal Encounter

Remember that guy who had his zipper down the first time you met him? No? Well, then it probably never happened. But if you *do* remember that guy, it's because he's impossible to forget! Research confirms that undoing the first impressions we make is nearly impossible, and if you're thinking of someone right now, it's more evidence to the point.

Because HR professionals are counted on to be credible activists in their workplace, they are always "on." There's never a moment when part of what we're doing or saying is not being tallied into a column marked "reliable" or "unreliable."

IN ACTION

The everyday informal encounter of every HR professional must embody "the integration of core values, integrity, and accountability throughout all organizational and business practices,"[1] as defined by SHRM's ethical practice in the Competency Model. To be a respected business partner (a subcompetency of SHRM's consultation competency), the HR professional needs to be a role model at all times.

This scrutiny means that we need to be aware of the impact we make in our workplace. We can implement everyday skills that help us make a positive contribution to our company each day, and in so doing, build our reputation as someone whom others can count on.

Don't Be Negative Nelly (or Ned)

One of the best pieces of advice we can live by is to steer clear of the pockets of negativity in our workplace. After working in a job for a couple of weeks, we know who is unhappy and who is not. Once we identify those people, we should treat them strategically. We shouldn't shun them (that will only increase their negativity), but we should talk to them cheerfully and at moments when they're not on a grumpy rant. And we should probably keep our conversations brief, before they teeter into a downward spiral.

Even if we aren't contributing to a gripe session, a passerby or person next door may overhear part of the conversation and peg us as part of it simply because we're standing there. We should avoid that image as well as that temptation.

Instead, we should be a positive, energetic force in our workplace. People are generally attracted to others who have an upbeat tone and who encourage others in their work. We should not be a phony or over-the-top Mr. or Ms. Sunshine, but if we have an eager-to-work attitude, we'll often find ourselves being offered exciting responsibilities and opportunities.

People also appreciate encouragement. In an era of self-reliance and rampant individualism, we may easily forget that most employee surveys report that employees would prefer more recognition to more money. Despite how people may appear, they want encouragement and will respond to our acknowledging their good work. So whether they are subordinates, peers, or superiors, offering genuine congratulations on a job well done is a habit that will serve us well.

Be Action Aaron (or Alice)

"We are men of action; lies do not become us"[2]—another great line from another great movie ("The Princess Bride"), this one spoken by the humble stable boy Westley to Prince Humperdink's six-fingered commander. It should be our mantra in the workplace. We need to become known for action, not for being the person whose, "Yeah, I'll get right on that" actually means, "I'll get it to you the day after never." When we say we will deliver, we need to deliver what we said we would deliver on or before the time we said we would deliver it. Nothing erodes credibility like an inability to keep our promises, so we need to be fastidious about this.

A subset of this notion of reliability is good eye contact. Though we should not stare trance-like into the eyes of every person we encounter, consistent, lengthy eye contact communicates that we are trustworthy. When we're speaking, maintaining eye contact shows the person with whom we are speaking that we don't have anything to hide and that we're not nervous; when we're listening, maintaining eye contact shows the person who's speaking to us that we are indeed listening.

In addition to doing what we say, being people of action includes engaging in bettering the workplace, which means becoming good at negotiating. People are often reluctant to change, even if the change will do them good. We need to recognize the factors that will make our workplace stronger and engage those issues with a determination to create a better place to work for the people around us. To succeed, we will need to focus on other people's needs instead of on our desires—or theirs.

When we focus on supplying people with what they need, negotiating for change becomes a win/win situation wherein we win because we've helped people, and the people we've negotiated with win because they've been helped. This takes a diligent and attentive eye that studies our audience well to recognize what they lack and what would enable them to work more effectively or efficiently. Knowing what *can* be accomplished and what is merely life in fantasy-land also takes a healthy dose of realism.

Avoid Becoming Long-Winded Loretta (or Larry)

The longer we work at a place and the more experience we have in our field of expertise, the more compelled we sometimes feel to tell everyone all we know whenever we're given the chance. Saying all that is needed and only what is needed is an art. And like all great art, it takes discipline and training.

Keeping our message simple is about two things: seeing the root of a matter and addressing it directly. This is difficult because life is rarely simple. A fog often surrounds matters we are asked to weigh in on, so getting to the root of the issue instead of jumping to conclusions takes careful probing. As

---

DID YOU KNOW?

Rev. Martin Luther King Jr. used language easily understood and familiar to his audience in his famous "I Have a Dream" speech. There's something to say for simplicity!

well, in probing through the fog, we inevitably discover other measures that need attention, which is why we are sometimes tempted to be long-winded; however, it's useful to remember that we cannot fix all the problems, so we should focus our energies on the most serious ones.

Always Be Ready Reed (or Rita)

The assumption that HR professionals are always "on" means that in addition to being positive, active, and wise leaders in the workplace, we also have to always be ready to give an account of ourselves. That is, we need to be ready to tell others exactly who we are and what we do—not in generic terms, but in terms specific to our skill set, personality, and specializations. Doing so helps us communicate our role to our subordinates, our preferences to our peers, and our value to our superiors.

Perhaps the best way to think about and plan for this kind of readiness is to say that we need a great elevator pitch. The term "elevator pitch" comes from the scenario of entrepreneurs entering an elevator to find a possible financier in front of them. Suddenly, the entrepreneurs are on—this brief elevator ride is their opportunity to make themselves and their business sound intriguing enough that the financier will want to invest in it. This scenario captures the importance of being dynamic and memorable while concisely delivering the facts needed for someone to make a value decision.

As HR professionals, we are often asked what we do or who we are—by those both in and outside our company. This is where our elevator speech is helpful. To be effective, we should practice to sound impromptu and natural. Almost an oxymoron, the idea is to practice the key points, but not sound rehearsed. In other words, we need to sound sincere. The elevator speech offers us an opportunity to give a kind of commercial for HR and to provide insights to employees about our role and services to the organization.

We first need to gain the listener's attention: A successful elevator speech should always have a hook. Beginning with something memorable (or humorous) will help give people a flavor for who we are as individuals. Then we should quickly move to the heart of what we want to communicate. Although the speech should be concise—less than 60 seconds—we shouldn't speak so quickly that we sound rushed to fit everything in. This means that we'll need to pick the most important points to make and say those.

As with the opening, our close should be memorable and creative. This is an opportunity to build trust, so we need to customize our speech for our audience. The speech for those inside our organization will differ from the speech for those outside the organization.

If we intentionally build our character at work on these four principles of positivity, action, wisdom, and readiness, then our day-to-day encounters will speak productively to the people around us. They will enable us to become a valuable asset to our company and a trusted colleague to our co-workers.

Endnotes

Chapter 1

1. David Grossman, "The Cost of Poor Communications," *The Holmes Report*, July17, 2011, www.holmesreport.com/opinion-info/10645/The-Cost-Of-Poor-Communications.aspx.

2. Towers Watson, *2009/2010 Communication ROI Study Report—Capitalizing on Effective Communication: How Courage, Innovation and Discipline Drive Business Results in Challenging Times*, 2010, www.towerswatson.com/assets/pdf/670/NA-2009-14890.pdf.

3. Debra Hamilton, *Top Ten Email Blunders That Cost Companies Money*, 2010, www.businesslunchandlearn.com/documents/SpecialReport2010.pdf.

4. National Association of Colleges and Employers, *Job Outlook 2012*, 2011, www.careers.uiowa.edu/leadershipacademy/NACE%20Job_Outlook_2012.pdf.

5. American Management Association, *AMA 2010 Critical Skills Survey*, 2010, www.amanet.org/news/AMA-2010-critcal-skills-survey.aspx.

6. Society for Human Resource Management, *SHRM Elements for HR Success Competency Model*, 2012, www.shrm.org/HRCompetencies/Documents/Competency%20Model%207%203.pdf.

7. The RBL Group and the University of Michigan Ross School of Business, *The 2012 Human Resource Competency Study*, 2012, http://rbl.net/index.php/hrcs/index/overview.

8. Society for Human Resource Management, *2008 Managing Your HR Career*, 2008, www.shrm.org/research/surveyfindings/articles/documents/managing%20you%20hr%20career%20survey%20report.pdf.

9. Towers Watson, *Capitalizing on Effective Communication*.

10. Society for Human Resource Management, *SHRM Elements for HR Success Competency Model*, 2012, www.shrm.org/HRCompetencies/Documents/Competency%20Model%207%203.pdf.

Chapter 2

1. David B. Ross, *Speech Anxiety Student Workbook*, 1992, www.clcillinois.edu/depts/vpe/gened/pdf/Speech_AnxietyWorkbook.pdf.

2. Society for Human Resource Management, *SHRM Elements for HR Success Competency Model*, 2012, www.shrm.org/HRCompetencies/Documents/Competency%20Model%207%203.pdf.

3. Ibid.

4. Susan A. Murphy, *Leading a Multigenerational Workforce* (Washington, DC: AARP, 2007), 27 http://assets.aarp.org/www.aarp.org_/cs/misc/leading_a_multigenerational_workforce.pdf.

5. Harriet Hankin, *The New Workforce: Five Sweeping Trends That Will Shape Your Company's Future* (New York: AMA, 2005), 64-87.

6. Richard E. Mayer and Roxana Moreno, "Nine Ways to Reduce Cognitive Load in Multimedia Learning," *Educational Psychologist* 38, no. 1 (2003): 43-52, doi: 10.1207/S15326985EP3801_6.

Chapter 3

1. Society for Human Resource Management, *SHRM Elements for HR Success Competency Model*, 2012, www.shrm.org/HRCompetencies/Documents/Competency%20Model%207%203.pdf.

2. Richard Dowis, *The Lost Art of the Great Speech: How To Write It, How To Deliver It* (New York: AMA, 2000), 116-119.

3. Jeff Davidson, *The Complete Guide to Public Speaking.* (Hoboken, NJ: Wiley, 2003), 49-53.

4. U.S. Department of Labor, Bureau of Labor Statistics, "Employee Tenure Summary," news release, September 18, 2012, www.bls.gov/news.release/tenure.nr0.htm.

Chapter 4

1. Society for Human Resource Management, *SHRM Elements for HR Success Competency Model*, 2012, www.shrm.org/HRCompetencies/Documents/Competency%20Model%207%203.pdf.

2. Harriet Hankin, *The New Workforce: Five Sweeping Trends That Will Shape Your Company's Future* (New York: AMA, 2005), 221.

3. John C. Maxwell, *Failing Forward: Turning Mistakes into Stepping Stones for Success* (Nashville: Thomas Nelson, 2000), 34.

Chapter 5

1. Society for Human Resource Management, *SHRM Elements for HR Success Competency Model*, 2012, www.shrm.org/HRCompetencies/Documents/Competency%20Model%207%203.pdf.

2. Dori Meinert, "Layoff Victims Won't Hold a Grudge If Treated Fairly," *HR Magazine*, November 2012, www.shrm.org/Publications/hrmagazine/EditorialContent/2012/1112/Pages/1112brief.aspx.

3. Joelle Jay, "Focus on 5 Key Strategies to Improve Communication Skills," *Managing Smart*, Spring 2005, www.shrm.org/publications/managingsmart/spring05/pages/story1.aspx.

4. Peggy Eddens, Class Presentation, Dec. 2012, Goldey-Beacom College, Wilmington, Delaware.

5. Alan Weiss, *The Unofficial Guide to Power Managing* (Foster City, CA: IDG Books Worldwide, 2000), 126.

Chapter 6

1. Society for Human Resource Management, *SHRM Elements for HR Success Competency Model*, 2012, www.shrm.org/HRCompetencies/Documents/Competency%20Model%207%203.pdf.

2. Ibid.

3. Jeff Thompson, "The Science and Fun of Nonverbal Communication," *Psychology Today*, September 20, 2011, www.psychologytoday.com/blog/beyond-words/201109/is-nonverbal-communication-numbers-game.

4. Kate Berardo and Simma Lieberman, "Strategies for Cross-Generational Relationship Building," 2007, www.culturosity.com/articles/cross-generationalrealtionshipbuilding.htm.

5. Howard Ross, "Do You Know Disability Etiquette?," *Diversity Executive*, November/December 2012, http://diversity-executive.com/articles/view/do-you-know-disability-etiquette/print:1.

Chapter 7

1. Society for Human Resource Management, *SHRM Elements for HR Success Competency Model*, 2012, www.shrm.org/HRCompetencies/Documents/Competency%20Model%207%203.pdf.

2. Paul Harris, "Harnessing the Zeal of the Millennial Generation," *T+D*, October 12, 2012, www.astd.org/Publications/Magazines/TD/TD-Archive/2012/10/BEST-NIIT-Technologies.

3. John C. Maxwell, *Everyone Communicates, Few Connect: What the Most Effective People Do Differently* (Nashville: Thomas Nelson, 2010), 117.

Chapter 8

1. Society for Human Resource Management, *SHRM Elements for HR Success Competency Model*, 2012, www.shrm.org/HRCompetencies/Documents/Competency%20Model%207%203.pdf.

2. National Federation of Independent Business, "Performance Problems: Don't Let an Employee's Poor Performance Affect Your Business' Performance," www.nfib.com/business-resources/business-resources-item?cmsid=22883#.

3. Daniel Goleman, *Emotional Intelligence: Why It Can Matter More than IQ* (New York: Bantam, 1995), 154.

4. Lois J. Zachary, "A Little More Conversation," *T+D*, October 2012, www.astd.org/Publications/Magazines/TD/TD-Archive/2012/10/A-Little-More-Conversation.

Chapter 9

1. Sam Leder, "Hiring & Keeping Salespeople—Part 5—Employee termination," *Furniture World Magazine*, (n.d.), http://furninfo.com/Furniture%20World%20Archives/3974.

2. Society for Human Resource Management, *SHRM Elements for HR Success Competency Model*, 2012, www.shrm.org/HRCompetencies/Documents/Competency%20Model%207%203.pdf.

3. Challenger, Gray & Christmas, Inc., "2011 Year-End Job Cut Report & Economic Outlook," news release, January 5, 2012, www.challengergray.com/press/PressRelease.aspx?PressUid=207.

Chapter 10

1. Society for Human Resource Management, *SHRM Elements for HR Success Competency Model*, 2012, www.shrm.org/HRCompetencies/Documents/Competency%20Model%207%203.pdf.

2. John R. Schermerhorn Jr., James G. Hunt, and Richard N. Osborn, *Organizational Behavior*, 9th ed. (Hoboken, NJ: John Wiley, 2005), 300.

3. Robert B. Cialdini, *Influence: The Psychology of Persuasion* (New York: William Morrow, 1993), 167-207.

4. Jim Rohn, http://JimRohn.com.

5. Guy Kawasaki, *Enchantment: The Art of Changing Hearts, Minds, and Actions* (New York: Portfolio/Penguin, 2011), 20.

6. Bernard T. Ferrari, *Power Listening: Mastering the Most Critical Business Skill of All* (New York: Portfolio/Penguin, 2012), 39-40.

7. Stephen R. Covey, *The 7 Habits of Highly Effective People: Powerful Lessons in Personal Change* (New York: Free Press, 2004), 237.

Chapter 11

1. Jack Welch, World Business Forum, Oct. 2010, New York.

2. Society for Human Resource Management, *SHRM Elements for HR Success Competency Model*, 2012, www.shrm.org/HRCompetencies/Documents/Competency%20Model%207%203.pdf.

3. Rick Gilbert, "Four Presentation Strategies for a C-Level Audience," *T+D*, October 2012, www.astd.org/Publications/Magazines/TD/TD-Archive/2012/10/4-Presentation-Strategies-for-a-C-Level-Audience.

Chapter 12

1. Society for Human Resource Management, *SHRM Elements for HR Success Competency Model*, 2012, www.shrm.org/HRCompetencies/Documents/Competency%20Model%207%203.pdf.

2. Marie-Line Germain, and Manuel J. Tejeda, "A Preliminary Exploration on the Measurement of Expertise: An Initial Development of a Psychometric Scale," *Human Resource Development Quarterly* 23, no. 2 (Summer 2012): 203-232.

3. Terry Bragg, "Body Language Affects First Impressions," *Business First*, May 2002, www.bizjournals.com/louisville/stories/2002/05/13/editorial2.html?page=all.

Chapter 13

1. Society for Human Resource Management, *SHRM Elements for HR Success Competency Model*, 2012, www.shrm.org/HRCompetencies/Documents/Competency%20Model%207%203.pdf.

2. "The Princess Bride," directed by Rob Reiner (Los Angeles, CA: 20th Century Fox, 1987).

Index

About the Authors

Patricia M. Buhler, DBA, MBA, SPHR, is a professor of management at Goldey-Beacom College and is the owner of Buhler Business Consultants. Pat is active in Delaware's chapter of the Society for Human Resource Management (SHRM). Her previous books include *Perfecting the Art of Management: A Comprehensive Guide to Organizational Leadership* (2010), *The Employee Satisfaction Revolution: Understanding and Unleashing the Power of a Satisfied Workforce* (2009), and *Human Resource Management: All the Information You Need to Manage Your Staff and Meet Your Business Objectives* (2002).

Joel D. Worden, Ph.D., is an associate professor of English and communication at Goldey-Beacom College. Joel consults with businesses and individuals to increase the effectiveness of their verbal and written communication. He has published a variety of materials, from study guides to chapters in a children's book.

Additional SHRM-Published Books

101 Sample Write-Ups for Documenting Employee Performance Problems: A Guide to Progressive Discipline & Termination
   Paul Falcone

Business Literacy Survival Guide for HR Professionals
   Regan W. Garey

Business-Focused HR: 11 Processes to Drive Results
   Scott P. Mondore, Shane S. Douthitt, and Marissa A. Carson

The Chief HR Officer: Defining the New Role of Human Resource Leaders
   Patrick M. Wright, John W. Boudreau, David A. Pace, Elizabeth "Libby" Sartain, Paul McKinnon, and Richard L. Antoine (eds.)

The Cultural Fit Factor: Creating an Employment Brand That Attracts, Retains, and Repels the Right Employees
   Lizz Pellet

The Essential Guide to Workplace Investigations: How to Handle Employee Complaints & Problems
   Lisa Guerin

From Hello to Goodbye: Proactive Tips for Maintaining Positive Employee Relations
   Christine V. Walters

Got A Minute? The 9 Lessons Every HR Professional Must Learn to Be Successful
   Dale J. Dwyer and Sheri A. Caldwell

Healthy Employees, Healthy Business: Easy, Affordable Ways to Promote Workplace Wellness
   Ilona Bray

Hidden Drivers of Success: Leveraging Employee Insights for Strategic Advantage
    William A. Schiemann, Jerry H. Seibert, and Brian S. Morgan

HR at Your Service: Lessons from Benchmark Service Organizations
    Gary P. Latham and Robert C. Ford

Never Get Lost Again: Navigating Your HR Career
    Nancy E. Glube and Phyllis G. Hartman

The Power of Stay Interviews for Engagement and Retention
    Richard P. Finnegan

Proving the Value of HR: How and Why to Measure ROI
    Jack J. Phillips and Patricia Pulliam Phillips

A Necessary Evil: Managing Employee Activity on Facebook, Twitter, LinkedIn ... and the Hundreds of Other Social Media Sites
    Aliah D. Wright

Stop Bullying at Work: Strategies and Tools for HR and Legal Professionals
    Teresa A. Daniel

Transformational Diversity: Why and How Intercultural Competencies Can Help Organizations to Survive and Thrive
    Fiona Citkin and Lynda Spielman

Workflex: The Essential Guide to Effective and Flexible Workplaces
    Families and Work Institute and Society for Human Resource Management